Bondage to Freedom

My 4 year battle
with porn and
how <u>Jesus</u> was
the only cure

Also By E.E. Cooley

<u>Prime Youth</u>

Prime Youth: Prisoners of the Masquerade

The Nameless Man

To all the no longer innocent boys and girls
To all who live in constant agony, anger, fear, shame, and depression
To all who hate themselves and wish they had a time machine
To all those who have so much shame it led to suicide of all stages
To all the parents who feel they failed their children
To all the parents who just want to help their children
To all the girls who suffer in silence because they were told sexual sin is a man's problem, not a woman's
To those who want to help their friends but don't know how
To those who want to scream their lungs out, but don't or can't
To all the restless, tear-filled nights
To those who repeated day after day "take it all away... please"
To all that was lost
To all that will never be
To all that was taken

May you let God set you free
heal you
and save you

Warning: this book contains graphic sexual content

Just because you can read, doesn't mean you should be reading this book. I wrote this book for three very specific groups of people. 1) If you are currently struggling with porn, masturbating, or any other sexual sin, this is your message of hope from someone that survived and found freedom. 2) If you are the parent of a son or daughter that you found out or know is struggling with porn, masturbating, or any other sexual sin. 3) The friend that doesn't know how to help, this is your look behind enemy lines. If you are not one of those people, DO NOT read this book. You do not need to have this knowledge in your brain if you have the choice. No one should. Only read this for the help it will provide, not the knowledge on the subject you could gain. I wrote this book to help others, to save others. Not for any other reason.

In Ecclesiastes 1:18 it says: "For in much wisdom is much grief, And he who increases knowledge increases sorrow." If you do not fall into the categories listed above, there will only be sorrow for you in this book. So before you leave, I want to give you one piece of advice that I will shout from the mountains until I die. DO NOT partake in any kind of pornography. Videos, magazines, pictures, whatever may be pornographic that comes in front of your path in life. And DO NOT masturbate. 1 Corinthians 6:18 tells us to "Flee sexual immorality. For every sin a man does is outside his body. But he who commits sexual immoralities sins against his own body." Run from anything sexual that is not you having sex with your spouse of the opposite sex. God doesn't tell us stuff just because. He does because He defines right and wrong. But He also is a loving God, a loving father who wants to protect His children. Heed His warning.

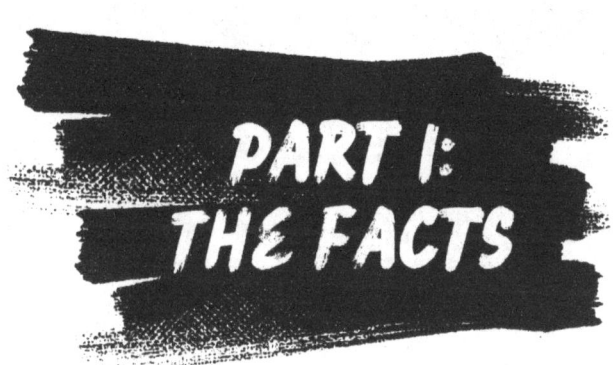

PART 1:
THE FACTS

WHAT IS SEXUAL SIN?

Before I can even think about telling my testimony and giving advice based off my experience, I need to get everyone on the same page. This includes what sexual sin is and some definitions. Because it surprised me when I heard it, but some people look at or read material that they never realized was pornographic. So I'll start with going through the Bible and listing all the different types of sexual sin mentioned, list and describe all the different types of porn, the definition of masturbation, and any other miscellaneous terms that I want to make clear.

Sexual Sin as Described in the Bible:

- Sexual immorality — an immoral act or practice relating to sex

- Adultery — sexual unfaithfulness of a married person (Exodus 20:14)

- Premarital sex — Sex before marriage (1 Corinthians 7:1–2, Deuteronomy 22: 23–24)

  ○ Marriage: "Therefore a man shall leave his father and mother and be joined to his wife, and they shall become one flesh. And they were both naked, the man and the woman, and were not ashamed."

- Genesis 2:24–25

• Homosexual (n – homosexuality) — of, relating to, or marked by sexual interest in the same sex as oneself; also: of, or involving sexual intercourse between members of the same sex (1 Corinthians 6:9–11)

• Bestiality — sexual relations between a human being and a lower animal (Deuteronomy 27:21)

• Incest — sexual intercourse between persons so closely related that marriage is illegal (Deuteronomy 27:20, 22–23)

• Lust — 1: intense or unbridled sexual desire 2: an intense longing (Romans 13:13)

Now you may notice that there is no mention of porn or masturbating in the list of biblical sin. That may be the case, but it doesn't mean that by their definitions porn or masturbation don't fall into the previously mentioned sin. I'll explain throughout the following chapters after I define porn and masturbating.

Porn — the depiction of erotic behavior intended to cause sexual excitement
• Still Image/Picture Porn — Pictures, art, and other still or captured images/scenes depicting sexually explicit or erotic acts

   ○ ex.: photographs, online images, paintings, sculptures, websites, etc.

• Video Porn — Video and audio of sexually explicit or erotic acts (what is most commonly thought of and referred to when porn is mentioned)

   ○ Youtube, porn streaming websites, DVD's, movies, etc.

• Audio Porn — audio of sexually explicit or erotic acts

   ○ Youtube audio, CD's, audiobooks, videos that only have audio, etc.

- Written (Erotica) — Literary or artistic works having an erotic theme or quality

  ○ ex.: erotica fiction book section, books, magazines, websites, etc.

Masturbation or Masturbating — stimulation of the genital organs apart from sexual intercourse, usually to orgasm, and especially by use of one's own hand

Now I define all of this because I didn't know any of this before I discovered porn. So when I didn't know something I would research it, which led to me partaking in whatever it was I researched. I define these terms that you may now have knowledge of these terms so when you hear them you know what they are, so you don't have to do your own research like I did.

Now for some miscellaneous terms. This is primarily for those of you reading this for someone else who are unfamiliar with sexual terms (as I once was).

- Orgasm — The climax of sexual excitement

- Ejaculate — To eject from a living body: specifically: to eject (semen) in orgasm

- Intercourse (Sexual) — 1: intercourse between a male and a female in which the penis is inserted into the vagina 2: intercourse between individuals involving genital contact other than insertion of the penis into the vagina

- Erotic — relating to or dealing with sexual love

THE STATS

Porn, masturbating, and other sexual sin are far bigger than any of us know, or want to admit. And the research out there is endless. But I will specifically be highlighting stats related to my story.

Porn Stats

Disclaimer: In all of the research found and used for this book, none of the research indicated what the spectrum of porn and pornography included, and if the participants were told what was included. However, by the language used within the research it can be concluded by words like watched, watching, and age verification, among others, that the research and the participants are most likely referring to video porn. As discussed in the previous chapter there are four different distinct types of porn, still image/picture; video, audio, and written (erotica). The only research to distinguish on this is the CovenantEyes research, but is only seen on one stat.

The following research comes from the British Board of Film Classification (BBFC) published on September 26, 2019:

- Majority of young people's first time watching pornography was accidental, with over 60% of children 11 - 13 who had seen pornography saying their viewing of pornography is unintentional

- Out of 2,344 parents and young people...more than half (51%) of 11-to-13-year-olds reported that they had seen pornography at some point, rising to 66% of 14-to-15-year-olds.

  ○ The majority of young people's first time watching pornography was accidental, with 62% of 11-to-13-year-olds who had seen pornography reporting that they stumbled across it unintentionally. Children described feeling "grossed out" and "confused," particularly those who had seen pornography when they were under the age of 10.

- The report also demonstrated a discrepancy between parents' views and what children were actually experiencing. Three quarters (75%) of parents felt that their child would not have seen pornography online. But of their children, more than half (53%) said they had in fact seen it.

This last stat is very intriguing that more parents thought their children had not looked at pornography, when in reality their children had indeed looked at porn. And the following research enlightens us as to how that could even be a possibility.

***

The following comes from research compiled by Covenant Eyes in 2018:

According to a survey by the Barna Group in 2016
- 41% of practicing Christian boys 13-24 use porn at least once a month.

- 23% of practicing Christian men 25+ use porn at least once a month

In 2003, 34% of female readers of *Today's Christian Women's* online newsletter admitted to intentionally accessing Internet porn.

According to a survey conducted by the Barna Group in the U.S. in 2014:

- 64% of self-identified Christian men and 15% of self-identified Christian women view pornography at least once a month (compared to 65% of non-Christian men and 30% of non-Christian women).

- 37% of Christian men and 7% of Christian women view pornography at least several times a week (compared to 42% of non-Christian men and 11% of non-Christian women).

- 39% of Christian men and 13% of Christian women say they believe their use of pornography is "excessive" (compared to 19% of non-Christian men and 12% of non-Christian women).

- 21% of Christian men and 2% of Christian women say they think they might be "addicted" to pornography or aren't sure if they are (compared to 10% of non-Christian men and 4% of non-Christian women).

- 28% of Christian men and 11% of Christian women say they were first exposed to pornography before the age of 12 (compared to 23% of non-Christian men and 24% of non-Christian women).

According to a survey by the Barna Group in 2016:

- 1 in 5 youth pastors and 1 in 7 senior pastors use porn on a regular basis and are currently struggling. That's more than 50,000 U.S. church leaders.

- 43% of senior pastors and youth pastors say they have struggled with pornography in the past.

- **Only 7% of pastors report their church has a ministry program for those struggling with porn.**

In August 2000, *Christianity Today* conducted an exclusive survey of its readership—both laity and clergy—on the issue of Internet pornography:

- In August 1999, 11% of the calls received on Focus on the Family's Pastoral Care Line were about pastors and online porn. One year later, in August 2000, online porn worries prompted 20% of the calls

In 2000, a survey of 564 pastors showed:

- 51% of pastors said Internet pornography is a possible temptation.

- 43% of pastors said they had ever visited a pornographic site, 21% doing so "a few times a year" and 6% "a couple times a month or more."

- 37% of pastors said viewing pornography was a "current struggle."

- 75% of pastors said they do not make themselves accountable to anyone for their Internet use.

- In 2010, out of the one million most trafficked websites in the world, 42,337 are sex-related sites.

- 28,258 users are watching pornography every second.

- $3,075.64 is spent on porn every second on the Internet.

- 40 million Americans regularly visit porn sites.

- 35% of all Internet downloads are related to pornography.

- Pornhub, the world's most popular porn website, reports that in 2017, there were:

  - 28.5 billion annual visits to the website.

  - 81 million daily average visits.

○ 25 billion searches performed.

○ 50,000 searches per minute.

○ 800 searches a second.

○ 4,052,542 videos uploaded.

○ 68 years' worth of content uploaded.

○ 3,732 pentabytes of information transferred (enough to fill the memory of every iPhone on Earth).

In 2012, 43.8% of adult industry executives and stakeholders believed mobile devices would become consumers' primary porn-viewing devices.

Pew Research Center's 2018 findings on the prevalence of smartphone ownership:

- 9 in 10 Millennials

- 85% of gen Xers (ages 38-53)

- 67% of Baby Boomers (ages 54-72)

- 30% of Silent Generation (ages 73-90)

***

The following stats come from Pornhub:

That last stat from Pew Research becomes even scarier when we look at Pornhub (the largest porn website) and their own stats. Yes, they post their own stats from the previous year about their platform. And they've been doing it the last ten years, since 2014.

The following come from their 2023 year in review:

- 91.3% of all traffic to the website comes from phones

  - In the United States, 93% of all traffic to the website comes from phones

Of all their research from the past year (2023) though, I was unable to find a total number of visits or unique visitors to the website. The only piece of information I was able to find was at the start of the 2023 report they state: "Every year, the Insights team and Pornhub's statisticians sift through data from billions of visits." It's ironic that this same statement is in every yearly report going back to 2021. The last time a number was given was in the 2019 year in review:

"In 2019 there were over 42 Billion visits to Pornhub, which means there was an average of 115 million visits per day"

It's also ironic that there is no yearly review for 2020, instead 10 articles were put out between the months of March and June detailing stats for the website during this time.

The following comes from their first Coronavirus Update compiling data up through March 17:

- It became evident that as people were spending more time at home, either self-isolating or working at home, that traffic to Pornhub had risen. Worldwide traffic to Pornhub was up 11.6% on March 17th.

- Italy was the first European country to close its borders and put into effect a nation-wide quarantine... The drastic increase of 57% on March 12 came after Pornhub offered free Premium service to all of Italy, an offer that was clearly well received by home-bound Italians.

For reference, Pornhub Premium is the paid monthly service Pornhub offers that is ad free and comes with exclusive content.

Here are some additional stats from the 2023 Year in Review by Pornhub:

- Visitor Demographics (worldwide)

- 27% (Age 18 to 24)

- 26% (Age 25 to 34)

- 19% (Age 35 to 44)

- 13% (Age 45 to 54)

- 8% (Age 55 to 64)

- 7% (Age 65+)

• Visitor Demographic (United States)

- 23% (Age 18 to 24)

- 25% (Age 25 to 34)

- 21% (Age 35 to 44)

- 14% (Age 45 to 54)

- 10% (Age 55 to 64)

- 6% (Age 65+)

• 36% proportion of female visitors worldwide

- This number has increased from 24% in 2015 to 36% in 2023

• In the United States, 29% of visitors were female and 71% male

Masturbating Stats

Ironically this first article is titled "Masturbation Prevalence, Frequency, Reasons, and Associations with Partnered Sex in the Midst of the COVID-19 Pandemic: Findings from a U.S. Nationally Representative Survey", which once you hear my story will make more sense why it's ironic that I found this article.

"In an article released on May 17, 2018, in a recent masturbation survey conducted by sex toy company Tenga along with research firm PSB, drawing on data from 13,000 respondents ages 18 to 74 in 18 different countries... 84 percent of us [Americans] admit to self-pleasuring — 92 percent of men and 76 percent of women."

The following research is from the Nation Library of Medicine published on December 27, 2022.

Women

1,958 American women were asked if they had masturbated (stimulated your body for sexual pleasure, whether or not you had an orgasm) [Definition given to participants] alone in the past year.

- 821 (about 41.9% of total participants) reported not masturbating alone in the last year

  - 12.6% (104 participants) did not masturbate because 'I'm in a committed relationship'

  - 11.3% (93 participants) did not masturbate because 'It's against my morals and values'

  - 8% (66 participants) did not masturbate because 'It's against my religion'

○ 0.7% (5 participants) did not masturbate because 'I can only experience orgasm from watching porn, and I'm trying to stop watching porn'

• 1,137 (about 58% of total participants) reported masturbating alone in the last year

○ 36.2% (412 participants) reported masturbating 'To relieve stress'

○ 19.8% (225 participants) reported masturbating 'If I'm not getting as much sex as I want'

○ 13.9% (159 participants) reported masturbating 'Out of sexual frustration'

○ 9.1% (103 participants) reported masturbating 'If I'm so aroused that it's interfering with other things I want or need to do'

○ 7% (80 participants) reported masturbating 'If there is nothing else to do'

○ 1.7% (9 participants) reported masturbating 'Because – even though I try – I just can't stop myself'

○ 2.2% (25 participants) reported masturbating for 'other reasons' ('Note "Other" reasons include separation from partner, don't have a partner, don't have enough sex with partner, pain relief, safest during pregnancy, reading a sexy book or watching porn, I wanted to, no reason, partner has pain during sex or other health issues, for prostate health, and sex addiction')

Men

1,784 American men were asked if they had masturbated alone in the past year

- 412 (about 23% of total participants) reported not masturbating alone in the last year

  ○ 20.2% (83 participants) did not masturbate because 'I'm in a committed relationship'

  ○ 13.8% (57 participants) did not masturbate because 'It's against my morals and values'

  ○ 9.4% (39 participants) did not masturbate because 'It's against my religion'

  ○ 0.7% (3 participants) did not masturbate because 'I can only experience orgasm from watching porn, and I'm trying to stop watching porn'

- 1,372 (about 76.9% of total participants) reported masturbating alone in the last year

  ○ 36.7% (503 participants) reported masturbating 'To relieve stress'

  ○ 31.6% (434 participants) reported masturbating 'If I'm not getting as much sex as I want'

  ○ 16.9% (232 participants) reported masturbating 'Out of sexual frustration'

  ○ 12.3% (169 participants) reported masturbating 'If I'm so aroused that it's interfering with other things I want or need to do'

  ○ 11.3% (155 participants) reported masturbating 'If there is nothing else to do'

  ○ 7% (97 participants) reported masturbating 'Because – even though I try – I just can't stop myself'

○ 4.1% (56 participants) reported masturbating for 'other reasons' ('Note "Other" reasons include separation from partner, don't have a partner, don't have enough sex with partner, pain relief, safest during pregnancy, reading a sexy book or watching porn, I wanted to, no reason, partner has pain during sex or other health issues, for prostate health, and sex addiction')

Erotica Stats

And finally, we'll take a look at erotica stats. There are not a lot of hard facts out there besides book sales. So let's look at one of the best-selling erotica books from the last decade:

According to the *Los Angeles Times* "The 'Fifty Shades' trilogy, which began with the 2011 novel 'Fifty Shades of Grey,' has been a publishing phenomenon. The books have sold more than 150 million copies."

That article was written on October 10, 2017. I don't think I need to explain that any further.

PART 2: LOSING INNOCENCE

MY FIRST EXPOSURE

It's taken me till chapter three to finally start telling my story, and there's a very good reason for that. First, I needed everyone on the same page about what porn is and various terms related to porn and sex. And second, I wanted everyone to be aware of the actual stats on porn and masturbating. Because throughout my entire four-year battle that started in 2020, I thought I was alone, and women were so lucky because they don't struggle with this. That men were the only ones who watched porn, and women had no issues whatsoever. That masturbating was a foreign concept, and I was the only Christian doing it. All of which I now know is a lie. So now we're all on the same page about what porn is, other porn and sex related terms, and that LOTS of people, men and women, struggle with porn and masturbating.

Now let me relive my past, and I pray by you hearing my story, it helps you in some way, shape, or form.

My first exposure to porn was in sixth grade, when I was ten years old. Now I say exposure because I was not looking for porn. I had no intention, or want, or need for porn. I was on my search engine looking at pictures of electric chairs (I still have no recollection as to why I was looking up electric chairs in the first place. Just the crazy mind of a ten-year-old), and there was a picture I wanted to see the website where it came from. And the next thing I know I'm on my first porn website. Now this was a still image/picture porn site, so there was no video or audio. And as much as I don't want to remember, from what I can remember the pictures only showed women naked from the waist up. So I never saw a vagina. This will be important later.

When I initially found this website, I didn't know it was porn, nor did I know what porn was. There was no recognition that what I was looking at I shouldn't, that what I was doing was sin. Yet I hid what I was doing. The screen would always be pointed away from others. I would sit in my room on my bed and look at these pictures, always ready with another tab to jump to when someone walked by.

The more I went to this website, day after day, the more bold I got. I remember one time I was in our family room with one of my family members on the couch. I was in another chair sitting sideways with my legs over the arm. My screen facing away from the family member. And I remember thinking "I'm looking at this right in front of them and they don't know." And this went on for a while. I don't remember how long, but it was not a one-time-event, I looked at this website multiple times.

And then one day, out of nowhere, I knew what I had been doing was wrong. Unbeknownst to me, that was the Holy Spirit telling convicting me of my actions. So I immediately went to my dad and told him what I had been doing (I asked him about this randomly before writing this book, and he said he didn't remember at all me telling him I had looked at porn and told him. I don't think I need to explain this except that is what the love of God looks like.) After I told him, he put more restrictions on where I could use electronics in the house. I could only use them at the kitchen table; not in my room, and not where no one else couldn't see what I was on. I don't remember much else of the conversation except that he was proud of me for telling him what I'd done. And after that day, I didn't go back to that website or any other pornographic websites. And to make it very clear I did NOT masturbate during this first porn exposure. I didn't even know what masturbating was nor had I heard that word. Just because you look at porn doesn't always mean you will masturbate or it will lead to masturbating.

After I told my dad, he did not treat me any differently (besides telling me where I could and couldn't be on electronics). He continued loving me. He did not do any of the number of negative things you've thought would happen if you told your parents you've looked at porn and/or masturbated. (Now that's not to say that your parents could do any number of those things you've thought of, because we are all human and we all sin, we all make mistakes. But don't let that fear hold you back from telling them. Especially those of you living in a Christian household.)

In James 5:16 NKJV it says, "Confess your trespasses to one to another, and pray one for another, that you may be healed." Another translation states "Therefore confess your sins to each other and pray for each other so that you may be healed" (NIV). I didn't realize it at the time, but I was doing exactly what God tells us to do; what He told me to do; what He told you to do. So don't be afraid to tell people what you've done. I'll admit that telling people and getting help is the hardest part of the battle, but it leads to freedom. And for those of you that have trust issues, that's something you need to pray about, because you need to tell people. Now I'm not saying go up to a stranger and tell them what you've done, hoping they can help. You need to tell someone who knows you.

If you don't have a relationship with someone you trust enough to tell them about your sexual sin, it's going to be a big hurdle for you to get over that fear. But if you don't trust someone, the only way for that road of trust to be open between both of you is for one of you to take the risk. Take a risk and tell them. If you don't trust someone enough to tell them about your sexual sin, tell them something else that you don't tell many people or haven't told anyone. Start building that trust. And if you can't or choose not to build that trust, then take the leap and tell someone. Because once you tell someone, you are on your first step to freedom. Even if that person doesn't offer any help, having the knowledge that someone knows what you've done lifts such a heavy burden off your back. Again, try your absolute best to tell someone who knows you well and who you know will help you when you ask for it.

For some of you, you may tell someone and it goes nowhere, they leave you, break-up with you, whatever the worst case scenario may be. If that happens, don't give up. Keep making relationships. Keep reaching out for help. And I pray for those of you that can't find anyone that God places someone in your life who wants to help you and won't abandon you.

JOURNALING

For some people hearing the word journaling may send a shiver down your spine or put you back in high school English, or for some of you you're still in high school English and wish I would stop talking about school and get on with finding freedom. But journaling I found helped me in two ways: 1) it got my thoughts out of my head and made them tangible. 2) It let me look back and see how much I had grown, what I went through, and let me look back on any notes I made to my future self. But before I dive into these points, you don't need to journal in a journal. You can journal on or in anything that allows whatever is in your head to be made into words. So that can be a journal, notebook paper, scrap paper, notes app, online document, etc. I personally prefer a notebook or journal. I have a couple of notebooks scattered around my room from various years of my life, none of them even half full; And that's because I'm not an avid journaler. I rarely do it, but when I do, it's normally during really stressful times of my life.

Now the main benefit I've found with journaling is I see that my situation isn't as bad as I make it out to be in my head. The devil loves to convince me that my situation is far worse than it actually is, or that I'm alone in whatever it is I'm dealing with. It also can help make sense of your thoughts if they've been swirling around in your head. Journaling isn't a replacement for talking with someone else about what you're thinking, but journaling does help me feel like my thoughts are now out there.

While looking back through my old journals for this chapter, I've enjoyed seeing how much my situation has improved. I love being able to see how far I've come and see what my life used to look like. Reading my journal entries has given me extra confidence that situations in my life will improve, and that I need to be patient and trust God.

Now I couldn't find a journal entry or a piece of paper with my thoughts right after I told my dad what I'd done. It could have been me mentally writing it down, but after apologizing to God for my sin, I told him the next time I saw a naked woman would be my wife. I also promised God the first vagina I saw would be my wife's. I was very intent to never see a naked woman again. I think I can remember thanking God that I hadn't seen a vagina, that I still didn't know what one looked like. Even though what I had done was wrong, I looked to the positive in the situation. And that promise stayed with me since I made it.

It wasn't until 2020 that I made a journal entry about my sexual sin and sexual struggles that followed. That entry was a journal that I started at the beginning of 2018. And with all my journals, I write my goal or purpose of the journal and date it. I now do this for all my books I write and any other collections of writing that I have.

(I will be writing word for word the journal entries I made pertaining to my battle with sexual sin. I will not be altering the original text in any way. I will however add additional words in brackets [ ] if a sentence is unreadable or confusing.) So this journal starts out with:

What I want this journal to be?

As of the time of writing this journal [it] is to be between God and me. This is not to be required every day but if that does happen then praise the Lord. This journal will be to write my thoughts about anything in. It is not to become a burden but a pleasure and retreat from the world. I pray that this journal brings me closer to God in the days and years to come.

-Ethan Cooley (Signed in cursive)

2/4/18

We can all say that as of the writing of this book this journal is no longer just between me and God, but for everyone.

Even though I initially wrote this just between me and God, I start out me 2020 entry with

Warning!!!

Sensitive Content

Ahead

This was on the page before the entry. I guess I was concerned about people finding this journal. But now it's a warning to all of you reading this. The journal entry goes:

1/6/20

Porn has been a constant temptation on my mind ever since our family won a laptop. For the first few months I was fine. The laptop stayed at the kitchen where mom and dad could see it. So no sitting with the screen facing a wall. A few months of this led to my parents trusting/being less strict. I could take the computer wherever I wanted in the house. One day I was in my room and looking at some photos. That link led me to a whole page of Porn. I initially didn't realize what it was. I just thought it was a page with photo album pictures. I was scrolling through when I saw my first Porn picture. I initially scrolled away, but then I went back. I continued looking through the photo's, my flesh craving more. It wasn't until 2 months later that I felt convicted by the Lord to tell me[my] dad what I was doing. To my amazement, my parents were very loving on me. I believe their support and prayer strengthened my mind against the devil's temptations. From that point on, my mind has never been the same. There would be nights where I would continue picturing the pictures I saw in my mind. I would go few weeks thinking about the photos, then I would see it was wrong and repent to the Lord for me[my] sins. This would happen again and again over the coming years. That was until I get[got] my first smartphone the second half a sophomore year. This phone has exposed me to so much more than I could ever imagine. Instagram started it. There were no censored warnings. I would see photos, then go to the page/account, then go to other accounts. Then I started seeing things on youtube. These weren't just pictures, these were graphic, audible inappropriate videos. And today I hit my breaking point. I watched the most graphic audible and inappropriate sexual video yet. I feel unworthy of God while writing this. I just want to curl up and not do anything. But you know what my first reaction was to do after this? I prayed to God. I also asked my friend to pray for me. I didn't tell her what I had done, I just told her I was going through a struggle and needed prayer to look to God for help. And I know her prayer worked, because I am going to delete the instagram app. This will eliminate the temptation to endlessly scroll and find inappropriate pictures. But you know what I find a miracle through all of this. The Lord has protected my eyes from seeing a vagina. I truly believe this to be a miracle with the amount of porn I've look at. If you're reading this I want you to know that miracles still happen. God is alive and working in every human being on this earth. I heard a story about a husband, that before he was married, had looked at Porn. When he told his wife [should be girlfriend] she broke down crying. The Lord then cleansed his mind, and his girlfriend still loved him. They ended up marrying each other. God can save YOU! No matter how far you've fallen from him. He will always pick you back up. Your faith will be rewarded.

I had completely forgotten the mental battle I faced after my first exposure to porn. Those images I saw didn't go away. They popped up in my mind daily initially. Writing this now, those images are flashing through my brain once again.

I remember as I would lay in bed trying to fall asleep, I would take those images and imagine it not as a picture but as a scene. And that would consume my mind until I fell asleep.

The farther I got away from my first exposure I remember those images no longer being enough to satisfy the craving my mind and flesh had. So I would let my mind wonder beyond the images, which from what I can remember wasn't too far because the only sexual content my brain knew was just images. But I do remember fantasizing and letting my brain wonder into sinful thoughts.

I also forgot I reached out to a friend, but at the same time, I really didn't. Telling someone you need general prayer vs. telling them exactly what you need prayer for are two completely different things. Because if you're asking for prayer about sin, like I stated before, the Bible tells us to confess that sin, not hide it. I'm not saying that my friend praying was pointless, but that I believe there is a greater impact spiritually when we confess our sins; whether that's true or not, the Bible tells us to do it, so if we claim to follow Jesus, then we need to be confessing our sins.

Now about what I was looking at, again, I don't really remember. I only remember everything a month after the 2020 lockdowns. But by this journal entry, we can deduce two things: 1) I didn't see a vagina. 2) It was graphic relative to what I had seen up to that point. The only thing I can remember is that I didn't look at "porn" (or the typical video porn you think of when you hear the word porn). Whatever it was I didn't see a vagina, and at the time, I thought it was graphic. What matters most here though is that I recognized what I was doing was wrong (Holy Spirit Conviction), talked to God about it (I didn't write it, but I would assume when talking to God I repented seeing as I asked someone for prayer), "told" someone what I was doing, and took steps to remove that temptation from my life.

These are the most basic but most critical and necessary steps to find freedom. Not telling people is what I believed caused my second wave of porn to be four years. Which leads perfectly into how this second wave even started.

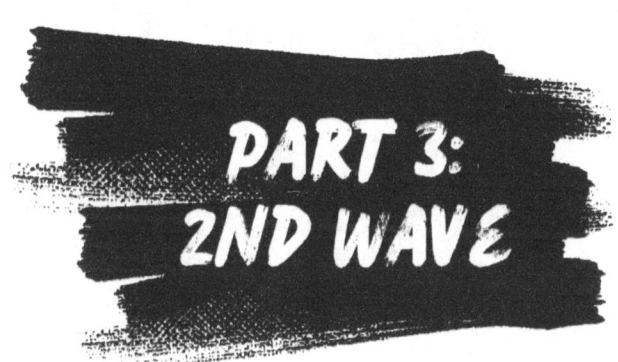

PART 3:
2ND WAVE

HOW IT STARTED

I got the call while sitting watching TV after dinner on Thursday, March 12, 2020. The next day of school would be online or packet work. Then after the two-week spring break that followed, the school would reevaluate if it was safe to come back to school. Their reevaluation took a heavy turn when we were forced into lockdown by the government. Now when the lockdowns were initially mandated and I found out all my schoolwork would be online, I was actually ecstatic, as was the majority of every other school student in the US. With all this extra time on my hands, I could catch up on various tasks I had fallen behind on and start some new stuff. Becoming addicted to porn and learning to masturbate were NOT on that list.

So after a month of finishing "everything" I wanted to do, I dove more into my erotic behavior and discovered what masturbating was. At the time I didn't know the name of what I had been looking at, but I was reading erotica (to recap, erotica is erotic or sexual literature). And I would do this on my phone either in my bed where no one could see my screen, or in the bathroom. I can't remember which kind of erotica I was looking at when I found out about masturbating, whether it was fiction or non-fiction. And for reference, non-fiction erotica are things like sex ed or sex-help books. While fiction erotica is made up characters and situations that involve descriptive sex scenes (the erotica section at bookstores would be fiction erotica). If I had to take a guess, it was probably non-fiction erotica. But when I discovered what masturbating was and how to do it, I immediately wanted to try it. Because at the time it didn't make any sense. I didn't know or think you could do anything related to sex unless you were having sex with your spouse. (Here's my innocence starting to wear away more.) So the morning of or the morning after I found out how to masturbate, I took a shower and masturbated for the first time.

And as soon as I ejaculated, I knew what I had done was wrong. I knew because I started crying. And this cry I still believe to be my soul crying out. That this is not what I should be doing to my body. So as I lay there crying on the floor of my shower, I cry out to God for help. I had reached my breaking point. I hadn't been praying much for help with what I now know was my erotica addiction because I truly didn't understand what I was doing was wrong and sinful. I remember that day wasn't my best. I was upset, angry, embarrassed, full of shame, every negative emotion you could imagine was going through my head. But the biggest emotion I felt was confusion about what I had done, that led to shock about what I had done.

One thing I'd like to point out during this time is that my Bible reading was not very consistent, and my prayer life was consistent but pretty much the same prayer every day. So my cry out to God consisted of me just praying. Praying for forgiveness, that I would stop this behavior every day.

The next time I masturbated I didn't want to do it, but my flesh was craving to do it. And that's the same way I feel every time I did porn and/or masturbate. My flesh took over, and I was its slave. Once the thought popped into my head, it was happening, whether I liked it or not, whether I wanted to or not. And once it did, my emotions would go wild.

This cycle continued, and the more I masturbated the more helpless I felt. I would pray that God would take this burden away completely. And as my burden wasn't removed from me, I would get mad at God. I asked him if he was even listening to me. What I had failed to do, though, was actually listen to His Holy Spirit who was telling me what to do. As soon as I realized I was sinning, I knew I had to tell someone. The second that thought came into my mind it would immediately be swallowed up by one of, if not all of, the following thoughts:

- Nobody else masturbates. No one can help you.

- You're a freak for masturbating.

- You're an animal, look at what you've done.

- They don't talk about masturbating in church, you're doing something even Christians don't know about.

- God can help you, you don't need anyone else.

- You beat sexual sin before, it will just go away like last time.

- If you tell someone, they won't love you anymore.

- If you tell your friend, they won't be your friend anymore.

- You can't trust someone with what you've done.

- If you tell someone, they'll tell others, then everyone will know what you did.

- The people you tell will forever judge you.

- Why do you need help; you can do this on your own.

- You'll be this animal forever, so why bother getting help.

I remember those thoughts came roaring over me the most at that time on my birthday, about a month after I first masturbated. I fought so hard that day because I DID NOT want to masturbate on my birthday. I, unfortunately, let those thoughts and the emotions that they created get the best of me that night. I was so distraught after that. I just wanted a small victory. There had been days when I hadn't masturbated and/or looked at erotica before, so why couldn't I choose a day and have that happen? It didn't help any that I was graduating high school, in 2020 of all years. I wasn't upset with how graduation was for me. I had done a complete 180 on school from "loving it" to "can't wait for it to end." And I was graduating as an erotic reading, masturbating, young man with enough friends I could count them on my fingers. That's what I was. That's who I was. That was the young man about to go into the world. I was not the man I wanted to be, I did not truly understand my identity as a child of God, but my flesh didn't care, it had its own cravings, and I felt I would be its slave forever.

These thoughts quickly led to shame and guilt, as is a constant with my sexual sin. It's always present and always nagging, always letting itself in without knocking. Even while writing this, those emotions creep back in again. But I first recognized them clearly and could identify them over the coming summer of 2020. This was made apparent with what friends I had kept from high school (who both were a part of my high school youth group). We would meet up in our high school parking lot since everything was closed and on lockdown. If I had masturbated or read erotica the day before or the morning of our meet-ups, I would feel great shame and embarrassment. The various things that went through my head were:

- They have no idea what I just did.

- What would they do or say if they knew what I was doing?

- Please don't high-five me, you don't know what my hands have done.

- They don't know what I've done, how dirty I am.

- I'm living a lie.

- I say I'm doing good, but I'm dying on the inside.

- How can I be their friend with what I've done.

- They wouldn't be my friends if they knew what I'd done.

- I'd rather not be here with them.

- I'm so embarrassed talking to them.

- I'd rather be home masturbating.

And this happened not just with meeting friends, but going to parties, to the grocery store, and the hardest, my family. I was living with my parents after I graduated high school, and as I continued hiding in my bedroom or the bathroom, reading erotica and masturbating, I was terrified of them finding out. Even though I had told my dad of my previous porn spurt, I was embarrassed to tell them I was back where I was before. Though I was even more terrified of them walking in on me masturbating or reading erotica. The shame that would have come from that. I would stay up late listening for the rest of my family to have fallen asleep before I turned into the animal that was slowly taking over. Or I would wake up super early before anyone else was awake, while other mornings my flesh would crave to masturbate and my brain crave to read erotica so much I would risk doing it knowing members of my family were awake.

No matter when I did it, what I did, what I read, where I did it, I always felt great shame afterwords. I knew what I was doing was wrong, was sinful, but I felt helpless. So when I'd cry out to God and repent, I would ask him to take it all away. What I wasn't doing was taking the time to listen and obey God. To read the Bible. I didn't do this because I didn't feel worthy before God, which looking back didn't make any sense because I still prayed. I may not have prayed as much as I should have, but I still did it. Prayer is taking to God. I asked for forgiveness when praying. So how did I feel comfortable talking to God but not reading his word or taking time to listen to him? That's what the devil is best at, confusing our thoughts and making us doubt ourselves, who we are, and who God calls us. Jesus came for the sick, not for the healthy.

This cycle continued throughout the summer. I would read erotica and/or masturbate in my bedroom or bathroom. Or I would masturbate in the shower. Immediately afterwords I would be upset, angry, full of shame and guilt, regretful, and wondering how this even happened and how long it would continue. I'd ask God for forgiveness and have a crappy rest of the day because I was living in all the emotions swirling through my head. My actions didn't just affect me for a minute and then I was back on my feet, they stayed with me, craving more, to do it again. And that was all because I was running away from God instead of running toward him. It took me three years to fully understand this concept, because from the outside, it doesn't make any sense. But after finally running toward God, I can tell you he's right there waiting with his arms open. And there is no shame, no guilt, no fear, only peace and love.

So I'll end this chapter with my next journal entry a little over seven months later.

8/17/20

Yesterday was the first time in forever that I felt the presence of God. It's been 5 months since the pandemic hit the Earth, and that was the last time I felt him [Him]. I think this is the reason my life has spun out of control since the start of the pandemic. About a month into the pandemic the devil started tempting me, as he always does. This time he got me, and hooked me on a train that to this day is still going. It start[ed] a month into the pandemic. I hadn't seen anyone in-person in forever, I had done everything around the house and in my room that I wanted, and was getting really bored. So with my dulled mind, I gave in to the temptations easier than I normally would. I started looking through Amazon at sex related books, and looking through the preview of the first chapters. I would do this every day, always finding new things and looking back at the ones with pictures. After reading so many books I learned a lot a lot that I shouldn't have, like masturbating. I decided to try it one day, and it worked. I was so distraught and angry with myself. It didn't feel right, but I kept doing it. Because my flesh was master over my mind now. I was addicted to it for a time. Doing it every day one week. There would be days that my friends would plan spontaneous meet-ups during the pandemic. There were several times that I would be so embarrassed inside because I had just masturbated that morning. Those were the days that I really started to question what I was doing. So I went to God. I prayed for forgiveness, peace of mind, and stopping. But even with God, temptations are easier [easy] to give into. I would start going through the motions of masturbate, get angry, repent and pray, and move on. Every time I did this, I got less angry, got less concerned, and became desensitized to ejaculating. And it didn't help that from time to time I would go back to Amazon and look at books and other sexual content on the website. But then I went to church yesterday. I felt God for the first time in forever, and Pastor Ron spoke directly to my issue as to why I gave into the temptation in the first place. Humans need to be social, be seeing people every day. Man was not created to live alone. And to add to that, seeing others besides your family keeps you accountable. I got so sick thinking about if my friends knew I masturbated. I'm not afraid what they would do, I'm embarrassed that I'm essentially living a lie. I've not told anyone about my masturbating besides God. And today, 4 months later, I can say that God is helping me. I've been masturbating once a week for the last month or so. And yesterday, I prayed long and hard in church about being sorry for my masturbating, asking for forgiveness, and declaring that every day I would pray [for the] strength not to masturbate. If someone is to find this journal than I urge you to pray for me. This will be a battle until the day I die and go to be with the Lord. If you are struggling as I am, I want you to know that God has helped me. He will help you too, all you need to do is ask. I hope that from this day forward there will be a change in my life for the better. God, let me never forget that you always help at the right time, not the convenient time.

It's still shocking to me that I intended these entries to be just between me and God, yet I wrote them like others would read them, and now these entries are for you reading this book. But I do want to make one note on my entry. When

I wrote "God, let me never forget that you always help at the right time, not the convenient time," I have no idea what I was trying to communicate. I could have been referencing what we learn by going through trials and tribulations. Because we could be asking God to deliver us from our trials, but we go through them needing to rely on Him to get through the trial and will hopefully come out stronger having learned something. But God will always help you, he will never leave nor forsake you. But you have to be willing to listen to God and do what he tells you to do. Because if you don't, you'll never find freedom and you'll end up like me. Discovering porn. The porn you immediately think of when you hear porn.

DISCOVERING "PORN"

If you already read the first chapter, then you would know that I had already discovered porn. That would be still-image porn, or picture porn, as well as written porn or erotica. I put "porn" in quotations because I discovered the porn that most people think of when they hear the word porn, that is video porn. But we now know that porn is more than just videos. So when you hear the word porn, now you shouldn't think of just video porn, but also still image, written or erotica, and audio porn.

I discovered video porn about six months from when I first masturbated. During those six months, I had started looking online for help and advice to stop looking at porn. I didn't do this very much, but one day I found a video doing a commentary on porn, and they talked about Pornhub, the largest porn website on the internet. And once the thought to look up what Pornhub was, was in my mind, it was locked in. So that night as I "went to bed," I pulled the covers over my head, turned my phone brightness all the way down (because I was more concerned with not burning my retinas out than looking at something I knew I shouldn't. Once you start doing porn and/or masturbating, you brain doesn't make any sense.), and searched up pornhub. I knew what I was doing was sinful, yet I clicked the link that forever changed my life, because I was a slave to my flesh.

At first I was horrified, disgusted, and curious about what I saw when the website first loaded. The horror and disgust were the Holy Spirit telling me to stop, to put the phone down, no, throw the phone across the room, and run away from the situation. While the curiosity was my flesh and sexual nature wanting to know more, to have questions answered. So I watched my first porn video. At first I didn't know what my eyes were looking at. I was watching a man and a woman share an intimate act together that no one else should be seeing but God. Want to take a guess what else I saw? A fully naked woman, the very thing I promised God would not happen until I had sex with my wife. I even told myself, "That can't be. That's not what a vagina looks like. That is not at all how I imagined it. (I can't tell you what I imagined but it was not what I saw.)" That's how innocent I was. And yes, I grew up all through public school without seeing any female or male anatomy. My parents had me skip the sex video in grade school. Health class in middle school didn't show me anything (or I don't remember any of it), and high school biology showed my nothing. It was a miracle that happened to me. I could have had an innocent experience with my future wife when we had sex for the first time. And in an instant, I squandered all of that even further. The first fully naked woman I saw would not be my wife. My first orgasm and ejaculation would not be with my wife, but by myself and an online book, and now the first-time seeing sex would not be with my wife, but two complete strangers on my phone, and I wouldn't even be a participant in the sex but an onlooker, a gawker, an animal.

So I watch video porn for the first time and masturbated to it, and this started the insane battle in my mind. Because everything I had done before this point I had never heard in church or even in life growing up. So I only had the Holy Spirit convictions to go on. I knew it was wrong, but I thought I was the only person masturbating and reading erotica. There was not a doubt in my mind that video porn was wrong. I heard that growing up so much, even a couple times from the pulpit. But when I heard it, I always thought it was only one kind of porn, and that's what I assumed was being talked about when porn was brought up in conversation. In my mind I was doing something no other human being had ever done before. Yet during my entire three years I did not recognize that the erotica I was reading and learning to masturbate from were all written by other humans. The devil loves to make you feel alone in your struggles, even when everything and everyone around you is screaming "you're not alone!" I pray that the stats on who and how many people struggle with porn masturbating is revealing the lies you've been believing. And I pray that all the crazy things I've already shared and will share make you feel less like an animal, freak, or whatever else you call yourself. I pray you recognize alone you cannot fight this battle, but with God alone will you be able to find freedom by confessing your sins, repenting, and listening to God's instructions.

Because I did not listen to God's instructions, I was selfish and arrogant, thinking I could fight this battle on my own. Throughout this entire battle, there were two very distinct instructions that I did not listen to and ignored. The first was to tell someone (I first told someone two years after my battle started), and the second was to get rid of my smartphone. So after about a month of watching video porn and very quickly becoming desensitized to it (I was no longer disgusted or horrified by what I was viewing anymore. I was curious and my flesh craved more. I was learning more every day and couldn't get enough). It was during this time that I had a clear moment of thought, one that wasn't filled with what I had watched the previous night or that morning, or I wasn't thinking about what to look up the next time I looked at porn, or how I had masturbated. And after this moment of clarity, I wrote this journal entry:

12/4/20

A very cool day today. No, I've not overcome my porn or masturbation addictions, or my fantasy [fantasizing] addiction either. But the Lord is still working on me and has plans for me. Last night I stayed up till about 12:15, looking at porn for the last three hours. So I woke up not in the greatest of moods. Surprisingly, when I got a shower, non of the temptations to masturbate worked! Then in the middle of my class this morning, I got an urge to hug my Bible and pray. To ask for help first, and tell God I wanted to be different. I told him that right now I wouldn't be willing to give up everything, but that I wanted to get to that point one day. To give up everything to have these addictions out of my life. To be changed for the better. After that prayer I got a strong urge to buy a flip phone. Now I've been thinking for over a year now to get rid of my smartphone. It initially came during junior year when [name redacted] did a lunch and greet. We had these meeting[s] once a month during lunch where we would have Chick-Fil-A or Subway. Then we'd be randomly assigned to a table in the Falcon's nest[a small room off of my high school cafeteria] and have a group of questions to answer with everyone at the table. At one of these events, we got a question that asked what is one thing you would change about yourself, something like that. A few of the people, including me, said less time wasted on their phone. One girl, [name redacted] said she wanted a flip phone. I still remember to this day how she said she wanted one so that when she was angry after a phone call, she could slam the phone shut. But, back to today. So I did some quick research and found a Alcatel flip phone. As soon as class ended I headed out and bought the phone, using my 3, maybe 5 year old, Walmart gift card. The Lord works in ways you could never imagine. But the most important part of today happened on the ride to the store. I had one of Brandon Heath's albums on in my car, and it came to the song Light in me. And as I started singing it out loud, I realized the lyrics were exactly how I felt and how my life was going. And as I sang those first few words, a chill came over my body. Now it's important to note that I had on a thermal, thing plaid long sleeve button up, and my heavy coat. I was hot in the car, sweating. I knew immediately that that was God. It's also important to note that I was wearing my biggest gloves, and that I had considered wearing a significantly lighter coat and no gloves. It's crazy how things work out with God. So after I feel the presence of God on me, as I'm singing, I start crying. And I continue to cry song [sing], now turning into sobbing and sniffling singing. And in that moment of vulnerability and brokenness before God, I was so at peace. I never heard God speak audibly, but I knew He was telling me that He isn't finished with me yet, that He's always been there, and He will never leave me. And in that moment, I knew that getting this flip phone was the beginning of my healing process. Because all the porn I've looked at in recent years, has all been on my smartphone. The phone is small, has a high resolution screen, and I can look at whatever, wherever, I want. And after watching a few Youtube videos, I've found out porn is the root cause of all my other sexual addictions. Watching porn, leads to fantasizing, and fantasizing leads to masturbation. Without porn, I can't fantasize, which means I'm less likely to masturbate. And I learned about masturbation through porn. So it's all connected. It starts and ends with porn. Now, because I got a new phone does that mean I won't fall into sexual sin ever again? NO. All the videos I watched from Focus on the Family had stories of recovery taking over a year and more at times. No one was immediately cured. And I expect the same for me, because I'm human, I sin. But with God, I'm made blameless by the blood of Jesus. Recovery won't be easy, but admitting you want to get better is half the battle.

I find it so funny how I pointed out my phone had a "high-definition screen." My family wasn't anti-tech, but we weren't out buying the latest and greatest either. I guess watching porn on a low-definition screen wouldn't be as enticing to my flesh. If you have a porn video that's ten pixels, at that point that is just erotic audio (which is also porn). But back to the journal entry, healing starts when you surrender to God. He told me to get rid of the smartphone and look what happened. For those of you that have never felt the overwhelming peace of God come over you, it's an experience that's hard to truly describe except everything else doesn't matter in life. All that you can feel is an overwhelming sense of joy and the need to thank and praise God. It's an experience that I've only experienced while worshiping and praising through singing. And ironically (or scarily enough) I've always been singing in the car when these moments of peace consume me. I say all of that to say that in that moment of peace while I was driving to get my dumb phone, I knew my actions were what God was wanting me to do, what I should have done all along.

Now if you're following the timeline, you'll see that I'm approaching a year into my second battle with sexual sin, and I've said that this battle was four years long. But in my previous entry I said getting a flip phone and getting rid of my smartphone was the start of healing. At first that may not make sense, and I'll guess if that doesn't make sense it's probably because when you hear the word "heal" you think quickly or even instantaneously. The healing that was going on here was slow. It wasn't even immediate like I had been praying for. I had prayed for all the urges, temptations, thoughts, images stuck in my head, all I had learned, to just go away instantly. To go back to the innocent little boy who knew nothing. That wasn't happening, but healing was taking place, and the healing process could have been quicker had I listened and obeyed what God was telling me to. How much quicker, I don't know. All I know is that healing takes time. When you get a cut on your hand does it immediately heal up? No, it takes time. The bigger the cut the longer it takes to heal. The same is true with sin, all sin can affect us differently on a human level. 1 Corinthians 6:18 says, "Flee sexual immorality. Every sin a man does is outside his body. But he who commits sexual immorality sins against his own body."

The more I read this verse the more I understand why sexual sin hurts. It's not like other sin. When we commit a sexual immorality, we sin against our own body. The Bible tells us in 1 Corinthians 6:19: "Or do you not know that your body is the temple of the Holy Spirit who is in you, whom you have from God, and you are not your own." We are making our temple unclean by committing sexual immoralities, the place where the Holy Spirit dwells. And when we look at porn and masturbate day after day, we're addicted to it, but that's also a whole lot of sin we're accumulating. That's a lot of cuts to heal.

I say all this to make the point that healing will take time. As you'll find out later, even though I was healing, my situation got worse. But I'm here today. Because God never gave up on me, and I always kept running back to him. And he never has given up on you, nor will he in the future. By the grace and strength of God,

I have the opportunity and privilege to share my story. And I pray it brings you hope and restores your faith.

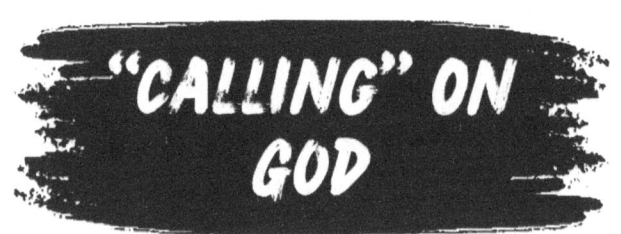

"CALLING" ON GOD

I have another chapter title in quotations. This time "Calling" is me calling out to God but not obeying what he was continuing to tell me to do. Because after I got my flip-phone, I still kept my smartphone, which God was still telling me to get rid of. But instead of listening, I kept it because I thought I was strong enough to not use the phone. How wrong was I. For those of you that don't know, smartphones that are deactivated (or can't make calls) act like a tablet. So I could still access the internet, which is what I did. But before I went to my smartphone for porn, I went to my laptop for a time. The device may have been different, but the motions were the same. Once the urge or thought came, there was no stopping it (which is not true. I'll dive into tactics I've learned to fight these urges in chapter 13); at the first available opportunity, I would watch porn and/or masturbate. I would feel so ashamed and repent, living in shame and feeling like an animal or a failure for the rest of the day and sometimes even into the next day.

Even though I was repenting, I wasn't changing my habits, so I was only just asking for forgiveness when I thought I was repenting. Repenting would have been getting rid of my smartphone, removing all portable electronics from my room, and believing God for who he calls me and not believing the lies of the devil that my actions and subsequent feeling were who I was.

It was around this time that I started to get angry with God. I was angry because I was getting close to a year from when I had first masturbated, and since then my situation had only gotten worse. I felt like God wasn't listening to me, that he didn't care, that he was ignoring my cries for help. When it was actually the exact opposite. I wasn't listening to God, and I was ignoring the help he was offering.

This was also the same for my Bible reading. Any Bible reading I did was whatever we read on a Sunday morning and the same chapter in John. John 7:53 – 8:12 about the adulteress woman. I thought if I read this enough, I would find something in it to help me. I wasn't reading the Bible on my own like I should have, like God was telling me to. So this became a next step for me to start reading the Bible outside of a Sunday morning and the same chapter in John every now and then. The only struggle with this was every time I would masturbate or do porn, I would feel unworthy. Unworthy of God; unworthy to read the Bible, which made it very difficult to start reading the Bible. I honestly don't know when I started reading my Bible again and how frequently it was. But I can tell you reading your Bible every day, even when you don't feel like it for any reason, absolutely changes your life. And it changes your life for the better.

After the initial end of my four-year battle at the beginning of 2023, I started reading my Bible daily. And for me that involved reading at least one chapter a day and praying. On the weekends, I would read more since I didn't have work in the morning. But there were some days where I wouldn't read my Bible in the morning. And the majority of the time those would be my worst days. Even though I would still pray throughout the day, I would still be in funks. It wasn't until I came home and read my Bible, followed by prayer and repentance for not reading when I should have, that I would feel ten times better.

The word of God is powerful, and you are never unworthy to read it. Just read Matthew 9:11-13 — "And when the Pharisees saw it, they said to his disciples, 'Why does your Teacher eat with the tax collectors and sinners?' When Jesus heard that, he said to them, 'Those who are well have no need of a physician, but those who are sick. But go and learn what this means: 'I desire mercy and not

sacrifice.' For I did not come to call the righteous, but sinners, to repentance."
And 1 Timothy 1:12-17 — "And I thank Christ Jesus our Lord who has enabled me, because He counted *me* faithful, putting me into the ministry, although I was formerly a blasphemer, a persecutor, and an insolent man; but I obtained mercy because I did it ignorantly in unbelief. And the grace of our Lord was exceedingly abundant, with faith and love which are in Christ Jesus. This is a faithful saying and worthy of all acceptance, that Christ Jesus came into this world to save sinners, of whom I am chief. However, for this reason I obtained mercy, that in me first Jesus Christ might show all longsuffering as a pattern to those who are going to believe on Him for everlasting life. Now to the King eternal, immortal, invisible, to God who alone is wise, be honor and glory ever and ever. Amen."

These two passages show us that Jesus came for the sinner and that he is gracious. So no matter what sin you've committed or how far you've fallen, Jesus is right there reaching out to you. One of the ways he's reaching out is His Word, the Bible.

Reading the Bible has helped me in so many ways, and it will help you too. All you need to do is read it. You can't go wrong where you decide to read. But if you're wanting material specifically on sexual sin, I recommend 1 Corinthians. Chapters 5-6 specifically talk about sexual immoralities while chapter 7 covers sexual immorality along with marriage. I have memorized the most scripture from 1 Corinthians pertaining to sexual immorality, which I will talk about later. But read something, I only recommend staying away from Song of Solomon, as that talks about two lovers and their story before and after getting married, including the wedding night. Which for some people may be a turn on or temptation. I suggest using caution when reading anything pertaining to sex, sexuality, and sexual immoralities, but heavy caution is put on Song of Solomon if you are actively addicted to any kind of sexual sin. But Song of Solomon does paint a picture of how God intended sex, within marriage, to play out. Which is what we should all strive for, even if we've lived or are living in sexual sin. Because when we repent and ask for forgiveness, God forgives us. And he also tells us to confess those sins to one another. Something I didn't do for well over two years into my battle.

CONTINUED ANGUISH

Between January of 2021 and the spring of 2022 my life definitely got worse. My mood, my productivity, my motivation to write, and every other facet of my life. I can say without a doubt in my mind that my sexually immoral actions were responsible for how crap my life was.

We've already discussed my lack of Bible reading and prayer, my anger toward God, the self-doubt, the names I called myself. All those continued and became worse some days. While other days they regressed. But they were always there, whether I wanted to admit it or not.

And I hate to admit it, but the kind of video porn I did became worse. Now you may be asking, "How can you do worse porn? Porn is porn, it's all bad." And if we look at porn through the lens of sin then you are right. Sin is sin, doesn't matter if it's a lie or looking at porn. Sin is all the same in God's eyes. Sin separates us from God. And as we discussed in chapter 6 from 1 Corinthians 6:18, sexual sin affects our earthly bodies, our temple for the Holy Spirit who dwells inside of those who accept Jesus as their Lord and Savior. So by that understanding, porn is all bad. But if we look at it through the lens of man, who you know has a hierarchy of bad things to do in this life. If you ask someone which is worse, stealing a candy bar or murdering someone, you know which one is without a doubt going to win.

The same can be applied to video porn. Because there is a whole slew of video porn out there to watch. It's not just a man and woman having sex; my "worse" porn involved me going from watching people have vaginal sex (Penis-in-vagina intercourse) to watching female homosexual (or lesbian) sex; sex that included hitting or slapping; and orgies.

So... yeah. That was a sentence. It was technically a compound sentence for those of you that still remember your high school English classes. (I'm hoping that last sentence made you laugh; or at least chuckle. I know this isn't the easiest book to read, but I hope my quips and humor sprinkled in make your reading experience a little more bearable. I also hope it lets you know that you can recover from this sin and be yourself again. That you can talk about how you watched homosexual sex in one paragraph and make a joke about sentence structure the very next). For some of you, you can raise your hand and say, "Yep, I've watched all of those." For others you may say, "I've only watched a couple of those." Others may say, "Nope, I've not watched any of those." Others may say, "I didn't see these acts you described with my eyes, but I read about them in erotic text, read them described or acted out in detail." Or "I heard about the erotic acts in erotic audio also described and/or acted out." While some may even say, "What you did was disgusting" and at one point in my life those acts were disgusting to me. But the more I did porn the more desensitized I became to it, the less it bothered me, to the point where hardly anything bothered me. I do remember watching some video porn that didn't bother me except one video where someone was hitting and slapping their partner during sex. That still makes me cringe. Praise God for that! Praise God that even in my sin I can recognize something is wrong thanks to the Holy Spirit.

Now you may be asking, if that bothers you, why do you keep watching it. This is what happens during an addiction. You want to stop but you don't. Stuff bothers you but you do it anyway. I'm sure there's some neurological study out there to better prove my point, but just know that once my addiction with porn started, all bets were off. I will say the only thing I did not watch was male homosexual (or gay) porn. I did have my limits.

But that is one of the hardest things I've learned throughout this battle, is looking for the positive in the middle of all the negative. Finding the beautiful in all the filthiness. The Bible tells us in Isiah 40:29 – "He gives power to the weak, And those who have no might He increases strength." God will always use our failures for his glory. For example, you did porn, ok, now what can you learn from it. What caused you to partake, what can you do different next time, etc. (I will talk more about tactics and learning from out failures more in depth in chapter 13.)

Now during this time, I was recognizing what I was doing was wrong, was sin. I was recognizing what I could change, but I wasn't doing it. Because there was so much shame and guilt surrounding me that I thought I would never change, that this is how I would be for the rest of my life. I continued to believe the lies of the enemy.

Now there were a couple of moments where I was able to write a journal entry about my experiences during this time; the first time being in June of 2021:

6/9/21

Yesterday I had a miracle happen to me. When I woke up yesterday morning and laid in bed for a while, long enough that I started thinking about porn. It then turned into me waiting to watch porn. It was about 9:30am, but I got up to check that my mom was gone. She wasn't. So I got up to say good morning, with the intent to watch porn as soon as she left. But before she left I had a clear moment of thinking and asked God for help. I was being tempted after this prayer, but got the idea to go out to the store. So shortly after my mom left I headed out to three stores, coming home to look for a coupon at one point. I ended up being out until about 1:15pm. The whole time I was out I wasn't tempted. When I got home I was tempted again, so I asked God for help and thanked him for the morning and not giving in to the temptation. Now up to this point, whenever I was tempted with anything related to porn, I would end up watching it that night and/or the next morning. Last night and this morning though that didn't happen! I believe this is my first step toward recovery. I think I thanked God about 50 times before I went to bed for that miracle.

At the time of writing that journal entry I hadn't read or memorized the verse from 1 Corinthians that describes exactly what I did. 1 Corinthians 6:18 – "Flee sexual immorality. Every sin that a man does is outside the body, but he who commits sexual immorality sins against his own body." The longer that I live and say this verse in my head or read it, the more God reveals to me. First off, flee is a very direct word. It's described in the Merriam-Webster Dictionary as follows:

1: to run away often from danger or evil

2: Vanish

3: to run away from: SHUN

This is the only sin in the Bible where the word flee is used to describe how you should react to the sin. And according to my journal entry, that is exactly what I did. And that's exactly what you should do when you encounter a sexual temptation of any kind.

Now the rest of the verse is a very interesting one to me. Paul, the author of 1 Corinthians, says every sin, that means any other sin the Bible describes, does not affect the sinner's body directly. But the second you commit a sexual immorality, or sexual sin, it directly affects your own body. And that's crazy to think about. That every time you lie, steal, cheat, get angry, don't love, are not patient, are not kind, don't listen to God, and any other sin you can think of, is outside of you. But sexual immorality affects you directly, your body. The more I read that one day the Lord reminded me of the verse about your body being a temple for the Holy Spirit. That once we accept God as our Lord and Savior, the Holy Spirit comes to live inside of us. I didn't know where this verse was, but I had heard it enough that I knew it pretty well. I looked it up while writing this paragraph and was shocked to find that that verse was the very next verse after verse 18. 1 Corinthians 6:19 –

"Or do you not know that your body is the temple of the Holy Spirit who is in you, whom you have from God, and you are not your own." I had read verse 19 before but never recognized that was the verse I had been looking for, for so long. BOOM! I'm receiving revelation and understanding while I'm writing this book. I honestly didn't expect that to happen. God is so good like that. You're writing a book about your past thinking you've learned your lessons already, and God lays downs some more revelation in front of you and keeps teaching you lessons. Hallelujah.

Now back to verse 18. The more I read this verse the more I understand why sexual sin is so hard to break. Verse 18 tells us it affects us differently than all other sin, differently being it affects our body while all other sin doesn't. And in verse 19, Paul tells us our bodies are where the Holy Spirit dwells. Let that sink in for a second. When we commit sexual sin, it affects our body, which is a temple, a temple in where the Holy Spirit dwells.

Writing this I thought of a story to help describe this. Think of your body, your temple, as your church or gathering place that you worship God at. Imagine you are inside worshiping and there's a storm outside that blows open the windows and doors. You would close those doors and windows before they disrupt your worship, letting rain and debris inside. If you leave them open, you are making a needless mess that will have to be cleaned up. Now think about when you commit a sexual sin. Those doors and windows are being opened and disrupting your place of worship. There will be a little clean up if you close the doors (repent and ask for forgiveness), but if you leave the doors open (keep sinning and/or don't repent and ask for forgiveness) then you will have a lot bigger mess on your hands whenever you decide to do with it.

I would even take this example one step further and say that when you commit a sexual sin, you start to create cracks in the walls of your church. A building has certain places where you can enter and exit. The walls keep anything from getting in. If it wants to get in, it has to go through a door. But these new cracks, your sexual sin, allow for things to get through the cracks. And eventually the cracks get so big, parts of the wall fall off. You now have holes in your walls; entrances for other things to get inside. The Bible compares Jesus' second coming as a wedding. The bride is getting ready for the groom, the bride being the Church, all people who profess Jesus as their savior. And the more I think about this comparison the more I realize why sexual sin hits us and affects us so differently, and many will say harder than other sin. At a wedding, the bride and the groom agree to the covenant of marriage. To be loyal to each other only, and no other. On the wedding night, the bride and groom have sex to consecrate the marriage. In a marriage the bride and groom know each other intimately. Like in chapter 1 where in Genesis God describes marriage as "the two become one flesh." If the second coming of Jesus is compared to a marriage, where we will know God intimately, where we will all be one, joined together and united in Heaven, it makes perfect sense why sexual sin affects us differently, so much deeper. A marriage on earth is a representation of what it will be like when Jesus comes back. It's a representation of His love for us, how much He cares about us, how He cares to know us intimately and we know Him intimately.

Which makes this perfect ground for the devil to tempt us. To twist our thoughts, to make us seem unworthy, flawed, an animal, shameful. The devil wants to destroy the picture of marriage that shows how much God loves us, and what we can hope for when His son returns. And the devil doesn't have to do that once the marriage has started, he starts that as early as possible. In chapter 2 we learned that children are exposed to porn at the age of 11 and sometimes younger. The devil doesn't care how old you are to destroy the picture of God's love for us. Because if we go through life having a skewed image of marriage and sexuality, it will affect how we see God. If we view marriage through the lens of shame and guilt that comes from sexual sin, then we will come to God with shame and guilt. If we view marriage through the lens of hope, joy, and intimacy, then that is how we will come to God.

God uses the marriage picture to show us how much he loves us, that he will never leave us. Just like a covenant in marriage. He's not going to go away with another bride, with someone else. He is in covenant with the Church, with you.

But now think about every time you've masturbated. Instead of sharing the act of sex with your spouse, you do it with yourself. You are selfish, not able to wait for your spouse. Think back to the church with the cracks in it every time you commit a sexual sin. Every time you masturbate you are separating yourself from God. You don't want God involved. You are breaking the covenant and having a covenant with yourself.

Now think about every time you masturbate while watching porn. You are being selfish like in the last paragraph, keeping the covenant to yourself. But at the same time, you are also giving the covenant to whoever or whatever you are watching. If you're watching people, they are giving their covenant away to whoever is watching them. If they are spouses having sex, you are entering into the covenant with them. A covenant meant only for the bride and groom, you are now joining that covenant.

Now think about every time you read erotic text of any kind. You are entering into covenant with the text, letting the text sexually arouse you rather than your spouse. You are reading something, if it's fiction, that is fake. A fake covenant, a made-up covenant. Not a real one. Or if it is real, it is from the author's own covenant, or they too may be pulling from other covenants. And if you masturbate to this text, you are again being selfish, keeping the covenant for yourself, and not allowing your spouse to sexually arouse you.

Now think about every time you listen to erotic audio. You are entering into covenant with whoever is speaking. They could be speaking from personal experience, they could be speaking with another person, who may or may not be in covenant with them. You could be breaking into their covenant, breaking their sacred bond, but also breaking yours. And if you masturbate to the erotic audio, again, you are selfish, keeping the covenant for yourself, and not allowing your spouse to sexually arouse you.

Now think about the time you had sex before marriage, or you had sex with a boyfriend/girlfriend who you didn't end up marrying.

Think about the times you've fantasized sexually about anything or anyone that wasn't your spouse.

Think about the times you masturbated while fantasizing about having sex with your boyfriend or girlfriend.

Think about the times you masturbated to a picture of someone.

Think about the times you masturbated while fantasizing about a random person or someone you know.

These all create covenant with someone or something that isn't your spouse. Who would want to go into marriage saying "I do," while also having said "I do" before the wedding with other people, or books, or audio, etc. Why would you not go into marriage being wholly committed to your spouse?

Now think back to the church metaphor. All of these sexual sins create holes in the walls of your church. Where there should have been only one door for covenant with God, there is now a covenant here, a covenant there. Now add up all the times you've masturbated, watched, read, or listened to pornographic material, had sex before marriage, fantasized, etc. how may holes are in your church? How many covenants have you made that aren't like God intended. Can you do that, or are there too many holes to count? Or would there not be a church left because there are so many holes.

That is why 1 Corinthians 6:18 tells us to flee sexual immorality. If you write in your Bible, you might want to highlight flee, underline it, or in the margin write FLEE in all caps. God warns us that sexual sin has consequences far greater than other sin that warrant action when being tempted with it. Because at its core, marriage is a representation of God's relationship to the Church. And if the devil can mess that up, or make you doubt it, or do whatever he tries, at the end of the day, it separates you from God. And the last thing God wants is to be separated from us. He wants to be intimate and know us, and we should crave the same.

Root Problem

My next journal entry came a little over five months later. This one I discuss what I thought was the root cause of my sexual addiction:

11/16/21

It's been a while since this happened, less than a month ago, that the Holy Spirit revealed to me why I was turning to porn, masturbating, and fantasizing. It all goes back to having an unproductive day that I feel like falling into sexual sin to make up for it. To make sense of this lets go back to the beginning. It was about a month after the lockdowns had started in 2020 that I got back into reading sexual content. Why? Because I had exhausted everything I had wanted to do and no longer felt I was being productive. Fast forward to when I got a job and was looking at porn. After every stumble (that's what I'm calling when I fall into the sin) I would go out to the store and buy something. This again reinforces me wanting to be productive. I found buying stuff as being productive, that I wasn't wasting this time I had been given on earth. This then goes to what I think the core of the problem is. When I'm unproductive I feel I've not done my best for the Lord. So since then I have made it a point to do something that makes me feel productive, like I'm not wasting the time I've been given.

And that is the last journal entry I have about anything related to my sexual sin. It's actually the last entry I had until, at the time of writing, yesterday morning when I wrote down a dream I had. But to the entry, thinking about the core, the root of the problem, really helped me going forward. Because everything we do, there is a reason behind why we do it. Whether it be one we can recognize or something that is so deep inside us that we can't begin to figure out what it is, we all have a reason for everything that we do.

The problem with addictions though is that you could have started doing something for one reason, but once you got addicted to it, your reasons can change. For example, if you start drinking after a family member died, and you grieve so long you become addicted, once you stop grieving, if you ever do, your reason for drinking is no longer out of grief, but another reason. Maybe it's because you found drinking numbed you from other pains in your life, or maybe you like hanging around the friends you made at the bar or the store where you bought the liquor. Now with addictions there may be no reason, it could be solely a bodily need. Your flesh craves your addiction, or it needs it. I've heard lots of people that drink caffeine daily say they have headaches when they don't have caffeine that morning. Your body now can't function without whatever it was you are addicted to, or it can but at a cost, like pain.

Now for me, I was kind of all over the place. My porn addiction started out of curiosity with free time on my hands. That free time stemmed from me not having anything to do, thus not being productive. Now as time went on and I learned what masturbating was and then tried it, I masturbated to orgasm. It wasn't until I found video porn and coupled that with masturbating that my brain started linking the two together. I would go to porn to masturbate. Then it turned into I couldn't masturbate without watching porn. (I could, but if I wanted to masturbate my brain went "Let's break out the porn to do that," and it was very hard to break that connection.) So whenever the thought came to do one, the other came with it.

So it wasn't until this journal entry that I started to recognize these roots, and those roots started to change. As the addiction continued, I would do porn/masturbate as a response to having heightened emotions. So whether I had a bad day at work, or someone told me something that got on my nerves, or I was frustrated about not writing more than I was (more likely not writing anything), or any number of scenarios, I would turn to porn or masturbating. And I would do this for a couple of reasons. While I engaged in the sexual sin, I forgot about whatever was causing my emotions to be heightened, it made me feel productive because

I did something, and when watching porn I got to see people have fun, which numbed me even more to my own problems that made me turn to porn in the first place.

And since this journal entry, it's been a lot easier to identify the root cause when I fall into sexual sin. And I challenge you to do the same as I did. If you are struggling with falling back into sexual sin, try to identify what your root cause is. It will be a lot easier if you talk to someone about it, talk to yourself out loud about it, or write down what you're thinking. And once you identify the root cause or causes, start praying about that on top of your sexual sin.

New Year, New Troubles

Now around January of 2022 (we're approaching two years since the start of my battle now) I started getting extremely fearful of eternity. Just out of nowhere. One night I went to lay down to go to sleep, and the second my head hit the pillow, every fear of eternity flooded my mind. I wasn't afraid of the concept of eternity. John 3:16 tells us that believing in Jesus comes with the gift of eternal life. I was afraid of how I was going to fill my time in eternity.

Some of you may be looking at me funny and saying, "You're a Christian, why are you afraid of eternity?" I'm a logical man. I think logically. Everything has a finite amount of time on this earth. Our life, the car I drive, the house I live in, the books I write. They all will degrade and turn to dust. (Just like how in Genesis God made man from the dust of the earth, so will our earthly bodies return to it. It's a really poetic picture.)

So the devil preyed on my logic and it worked. Because my brain could not comprehend the concept of "forever." So on that night I tossed and turned myself to sleep, with my face in my pillow, praying for it all to go away. I remember falling asleep in this state of fear and panic, to wake up the next day feeling better. This reminds me of the verse from Psalm 30:5: "...Weeping may endure for a night, But joy comes in the morning." Praise God I was able to get to sleep. Praise God I woke up without any fear.

But that night started a violent attack by the devil on me. For the next four months, I struggled with suicidal thoughts. And let me be clear, I was not suicidal at any time during this, hallelujah. I did not think of ways to kill myself, I only contemplated why I was on this earth and if it was worth living anymore. These thoughts didn't come every day. Some days would be great, others would be hell. The days that were hell were most of the time when I did porn and/or masturbated (not surprisingly).

Some of these suicidal thoughts were caused by me thinking about eternity, panicking, and that would lead to those thoughts. While the rest of the suicidal thoughts were from the shame, anger, disgust, and unworthiness I felt from my sexual sin. And this would continue for about the next four months. Night after night of sleeplessness, sometimes crying myself to sleep, rocking myself back and forth until my body slept out of exhaustion, all combined with the shame and guilt of doing porn and masturbating day after day. It was a miracle I was even awake and alive during this time, that I was able to get out of bed and go to work, even if just to come home and watch YouTube or movies the rest of the day. But one day it became too much, and I had my first and only panic attack at the time of writing this.

PANIC ATTACK

March 18, 2022. This day had been a picture hanging in the back of my mind. I remember everything about that night like it happened yesterday. I was working the evening shift at my job, and I remember that day wasn't a good day, wasn't a bad day, it was just a day. At that point I had just become numb. I wasn't the same person anymore. The guilt, shame, name calling, and hate I had kept inside of me had changed me permanently. So that day I was living in the new me, this husk, a shadow of who God had created me.

I was cleaning the dishes when all of a sudden, I started panicking out of nowhere. For no reason whatsoever. I've since called times like this the cloud of fear, and this was not the last time it occurred.

So the cloud of fear came over me, and I started to cry; again, can't tell you why. I was cleaning the dishes while crying (there's probably some health code against doing this), unable to see from time to time because I had so many tears. Then I had to step away from washing the dishes, and I composed myself the best I could, but I remember sniffling and wiping a tear every now and then in front of my co-worker. After a while I got to go back and finish the dishes, and as soon as I got to the dish sink, I texted my parents (who I was living with at the time) if they could come pick me up. That night felt like an eternity.

So when they finally arrived, I was relieved, Because I knew I wouldn't have been able to drive myself home. My mom came with my brother, and I remember them asking if I was all right, but for some reason, I was more concerned about how we would get my car home. (My brother couldn't drive.) I remember my mom assuring me that the car wasn't important and not to worry about it. How right she was.

As we made our way home, I tried my absolute hardest not to cry. Because I was still trying to be strong and not let this nameless fear consume me. But the cracks started to form on the ride home. Once we got home and I stepped out of the car, those cracks burst. I pulled my mom in to hug her and bawled my eyes out. It was not pretty, every hole on my face had something coming out of it. We stood there for what seemed like thirty minutes, but it was probably far less. Eventually we got too cold and went inside, where I fell right on the couch and continued crying. And I did that for a lot of the night. As my parents asked me what was making me cry, at first, I couldn't answer their question. Mainly because I was sobbing, and the only sound coming out of my mouth were not pretty ones. But once I started to calm down to where I was able to speak without the need for a translator, I told them about my fears of eternity. And the rest of the night was a night full of prayer, more tears, and prayer from relatives. I can't thank and compliment my parents enough for how they handled that night. They immediately went to God in prayer over me, called up my grandma (who is an awesome prayer warrior!), and assured me that God was there with me through this. I remember saying (half crying, half saying, so it came out garbled and I had to repeat it) and I asked the question, "If God is real then why is this happening?"

Of all the things I could say about that quote, I think it pretty much speaks for itself. I was at so low of a point that I doubted God's existence. My brain couldn't comprehend and remember everything I had learned about God always being there with you, no matter where you are or what you're going through. My brain couldn't remember all the times I had seen God's power demonstrated before, in my life and in others. But after a long night, those doubts slowly started to go away, enough so that my parents felt all right to leave and go get my car. While they were gone, they gave me some videos from Kat Kurr to watch on heaven and eternity, which definitely helped to ease my mind because God's shown her heaven before (ironic enough, I went and looked up on Kat Kurr's website to make sure I spelled her name right where I found a Q&A on heaven. As I read through the list, I had this overwhelming fear or anxiety, I'm not sure entirely, of what I would be doing for eternity. And this isn't the first time, this has happened before. It's happened a handful of times since. Now this time I immediately started praying and asking God why this keeps happening, as well as praying over me 2 Timothy 1:7 – "For God has not given us a spirit of fear, but of power and of love and of a sound mind." And this is over a year after the panic attack. A lot of you are looking for healing immediately, or a miracle, when the majority of healing takes time. It's a process. Trust God in the process. Trust God no matter how long the healing takes).

So after a couple of her videos and some food in my stomach, I was feeling a lot better, but just bad enough that we broke out the inflatable mattress so my mom and I could sleep next to each other. (Men, you can still be a man and need the comfort of a parent in certain situations. It doesn't make you any less manly.)

By the end of that Saturday night, my parents had concluded that this was a spiritual attack to keep me from writing my first book. Because earlier that day I had sent off my first book, *Prime Youth: Prisoners of the Masquerade*, to be edited. So it was initially concluded that this was the devil attacking me to get me to stop writing books. However, after getting some prayer the next day at church, it was suggested that I get some counseling. There was a member of our church who ran a counseling program out of the church that we decided on.

I started my first counseling session with them and ran through what had been going on in my life, except I left out the part about consuming porn and masturbating for two years at that point. From what I did tell them, the counselor concluded that I had experienced a stress induced panic attack. This was from me writing my very first book, which I had barely told anyone about at that point, and sent it off for someone to critique it with a fine tooth comb. And I'm not saying she's wrong, because there was a lot of stress surrounding my book. In about two months from the time of the panic attack, I needed to have my book edited by two people, formatted, printed, merchandise created, merchandise ordered, and advertise. I was down to the wire, and I think we can all agree that played into my panic attack. But the majority of what caused it was my porn and masturbating addiction, which throughout all my counseling (about three months' worth once a week) I never once told my counselor. (If you're reading this I'm sorry I wasn't trusting enough to tell you. Having that piece of information would have been helpful to you.)

Now during my first session I knew I wasn't going to tell my counselor about my porn and masturbating addiction. And I think for most people they wouldn't open up with that on their first session either. But can I tell you those sessions will be far more productive if you tell them everything. They can't help you if you don't tell them what's going on. From the little things that you think are insignificant, unrelated happenings, big things, and things you'd rather not tell them, tell them all of it.

Now just because I withheld some information doesn't mean that the counseling sessions weren't productive or useful. I learned a lot of breathing techniques (because when your brain has more oxygen it doesn't freak out as much) that I don't use anymore but that's because I'm not as stressed or anxious as I was. But should that day arise, I have those techniques in my back pocket ready to use. All of them were just variations of breathing or taking deep breaths. The one I used the most was where I would take a deep breath in, slowly exhale, then say a Bible verse or a positive thought in my head or out loud. And I would repeat this ten times with the same verse or positive thought each time.

It always amazed me how much better I felt after doing those. It reminds me of the story of Elijah after he had built an alter to God that was doused in water and God consumed all the alter in fire. The prophets of baal had also built an alter calling on their god to consume their alter as well, to no avail. After God consumed the alter in fire, Elijah had all the baal priests killed. For this act he received a death threat and is so scared out of his mind that he runs away. After a day's journey in the wilderness, he sits down under a broom tree and prays, "'It is enough! Now, Lord, take my life, for I am no better than my fathers!" He then slept under the tree only to be awoken by an Angel who told him "'Arise and eat'" where next to Elijah's head there was a cake and a jar of water. This happened a second time before a forty-day journey through the wilderness. And for the rest of that chapter, Elijah never mentions wanting God to kill him. In fact, at the end of the chapter, Elijah anoints Elisha as the next prophet.

Imagine if Elijah had gotten his way. Imagine if he hadn't taken that nap. A lot of times, me included, we like to think we're being spiritually attacked. When in reality, I would wager that we just need to either 1) take a nap/get some more sleep, 2) eat something healthy and filling, 3) spend dedicated time with God. Whether you do one or all of those, I think a lot of the times we think we're being "attacked" is us not properly caring for our physical bodies.

All of that to say there is a lot that goes into the way we act and what we experience in life. So it's important to be fervently watching and analyzing every part of you for why you may be experiencing what you are. Prayer is a big help for this. Ask God to reveal to you what is causing your anxiousness, your shame, your depression, your suicidal thoughts. Some of you may be reading that and saying, "I can't go to God and tell him about my suicide or depression" or "Christians shouldn't be suicidal, Christians shouldn't struggle with porn, so I can't go to God."

First off, God already knows exactly what you are going through. Hiding, keeping something, or not admitting what you're going through to God is the most pointless and harmful thing you can do to yourself. We are broken and hopeless people without God. We need God because without him, we will stay broken. We are a sinful people who only by the cross that Christ died on, can we boldly go to the throne and say "Help me God, I am a misfit, I'm a screw up, I'm a mess. But You are not. You are the only way to purpose and meaning in this life because You created us, You love us, You know us, and You saved us. So I come to You with my arms open, holding nothing back from You. I will never fix myself. I need you God. Only You can fix me. Only You can change me. Change my heart that I would love what You love and hate what You hate. To recognize that I should not sin, that I should not live how I want because of Your grace. I should – no – I need to follow Your teachings. Why would I not follow the creator of the universe, the creator of me. Because without You the wages of sin are death. And why would I die when I can live. So I come to You to confess my sin. I die to my interest, my thoughts, my wants. I die to myself that I may glorify You. I die to myself that I may fully live because when I live, I am never satisfied, but You quench my thirst and satisfy like only You can. Forgive me of my sins, my transgressions. Make me clean, make me whole. Renew my spirit. May I realize this sin in my life is holding me back from what You have, is not glorifying to You in any way. May I understand the consequences of my sin, and understand Your grace, Your forgiveness. May I understand how my sin doesn't have to hold me back. That by giving it **ALL** to You there is freedom from it. And You do this all because You love us so much, so intimately, that it's beyond our comprehension how much You truly love us. Words will always fall short, but I would rather try than say nothing of Your love."

To deny or keep something from God, that again he already knows, is to deprive you of the freedom, joy, peace, purpose, and love that God offers you. So all of that to say 1) be honest with God, 2) be honest with people, 3) being vulnerable with people is hard, but worth the freedom and help that follows.

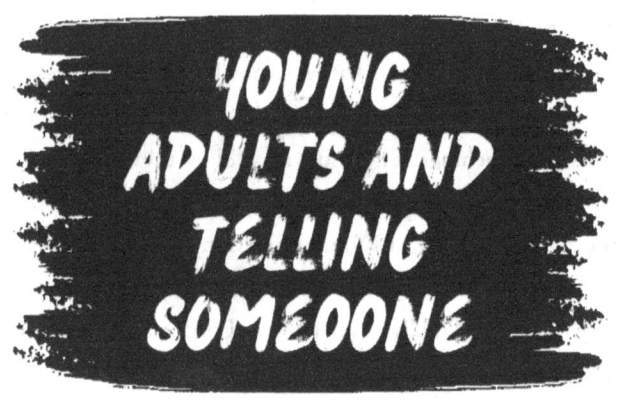

YOUNG ADULTS AND TELLING SOMEONE

It was during the spring of 2022 that I finally told someone about my sexual sin. I remember we went to a park and walked together as I told them what I had been doing. We talked and prayed and that was pretty much it. It was most definitely hard to tell them what I had done. But I think what was most disappointing to me, was that my erotic habits didn't change any. I was for sure that the opposite would happen, that my habits would change, or at least start to. But looking back, I realize now that the missing part to that was accountability. As you'll see later in my story, when I got some accountability, that's when things started to drastically change.

Now was telling that person worthless? No, it wasn't. It very much showed growth in me. That I was once too afraid to tell anyone, and now I had the strength to tell someone (That strength coming from God). So growth was happening in me. Change was occurring, just not the kind I wanted. Nor with the results I wanted.

<u>Young Adults</u>

Partly on my own and partly during my counseling it was decided that I needed to get involved at a church somewhere, for that fact just get involved with something where I was meeting other people. I wasn't involved at my current church beyond a Sunday morning for a number of reasons. And the Youth group I was attending at a different church I unfortunately decided to leave from starting my senior year of high school.

Outside of church during high school I was a part of two clubs. Robotics and Key Club. My robotics team was called Cyber Blue 234 which is part of FIRST for any of you FIRST alumni or current members. And Key Club was the high school version of Kiwanis or the Lions Club. It's a community volunteer club. Once I graduated high school, I kept in touch with only two people. Both of which went to the youth group I left. And once I joined college, it was a nightmare trying to make friends. I started college in the fall of 2020, which meant almost all of my classes were online. Because we were told to stay away from each other, the few in-person classes I had didn't go well in the friend making department. And the majority of clubs had shut down. The only one I joined was Circle K (College version of Kiwanis), and that was hard to do to say the least. So when I dropped out of college during the summer of 2021, I was going to church and going to work. That was my life. So it's no wonder why I would turn to porn when my life had, in my opinion, very little value. The two friends I did have went off to college and lived on campus, and I only got to see them on breaks.

So... yeah. My life was very bare before I joined my Young Adult group at Grace Assembly of God in Whiteland, Indiana.

I knew I needed to join a church group of some kind. I remember a year before I found Grace Assembly having a very heated argument with my mom about going to the young adult group at the church I was going to on Sundays. I basically made a bunch of excuses as to why I couldn't or didn't want to go. But I knew the whole time I should have gone. Because it would get me back in a community, but it would also hopefully grow me spiritually. So I did some searching online and was only able to find any information about a young adult group for one church in my area, Grace Assembly of God. I still remember it like it was yesterday. I played phone tag with the Young Adult pastor until finally connecting with him. I asked him about the group, and he agreed to let me come early so we could chat some more. (Tip to people who are scared or anxious to join a new group of any kind: It's not as scary to arrive early and talk with the leader of the group than it is to show up and hope you're not awkwardly standing around trying to talk to strangers. I did this because I was terrified of just showing up. This also makes it easy to introduce yourself to someone. You can say hi to the first person who shows up, or in my case, the leader can introduce you to the first person who shows up. Takes away a lot of the nervousness really. And if you're an extrovert, well... I'm glad you can go up and say hi to total strangers and make it look so easy.)

At the time the group met at the pastor's house on Wednesday nights. So I drove over early, talked with the pastor a bit about the group and my background, and since that late April meeting in 2022, I've been going to Grace's Young Adult group ever since. And three months later in July, I started attending the church on Sunday mornings, and became a member of Grace later that year.

Being at Grace is so fun. Every Sunday morning they say "Welcome home" and that's how I felt when I started attending. It felt like home. But it didn't always feel like that. When I first started attending, it was very hard to make friends. Was I a little shy, yes. Is it hard to go up and talk to brand new people, yes. My first time wasn't bad. People asked who I was and wanted to get to know me. It worked out well actually because the church had just hired a full time Young Adult pastor who was starting the very next week after I had joined. So the whole group was basically starting from scratch, and I didn't feel so much like the "new" guy, since everyone was now the "new" guy.

But that wasn't all that was making me nervous at the time. I had my first book to release in about a month. Things were definitely down to the wire, and with my recent panic attack on my mind, I was a little on edge. But things were on the up and up. I had joined a church group, was trying (trying is very generous of me to say) to make friends, and my very first book was about to come out.

So it's release day for my first book, *Prime Youth: Prisoners of the Masquerade*. It's now been two months since my first and only panic attack at the time of writing. And by the grace of God my first book made it out. I could barely sleep the night before, in a good way. I was so excited for the launch party. The event comes and goes as well as anyone could expect. (I had invited the brand-new Young Adult pastor because he was the only person to really talk to me and seem genuinely interested in me being an author. So I invited him to the launch party, and he came. So thank you, Mark. I don't know if I've ever told you how much that meant.) It was an amazing day. I may have set my standards a little too high though, as I was expecting, with all the people I invited. to have a line out the door, nearly sell out of books, everything an author could want. I didn't come anywhere close to that, but I also didn't sell just one book. So I ended the night a little disappointed.

Come the following week it's my birthday, and it falls on the night I have Young Adults. At this point I hadn't really made any friends in the group yet. And I wasn't one to just go up to random people and start up a conversation. So that night at Young Adults, no one talked to me. The only person that did was our new pastor for just a couple of minutes. I was really disappointed. I sat there like, like, I don't know. I just sat there all night. Luckily there was a movie playing so I had "something" to do. But for no one to talk to me all night, I was devastated. So that combined with the disappointment of the book launch, led to me being very emotionally charged. Which led to what, you guessed it, me looking at porn and masturbating. If you asked me during my three-year addiction when I looked at porn or masturbated, I couldn't tell you the day, just that I had probably done it at least once that week. But there are some events, like my birthday, that stick out to me.

But after that day, I slowly started making friends in the group and eventually didn't go to Young Adults thinking "who's going to talk to me tonight, if anyone."

Now it's "Who am I going to talk to because I know so many people." But I can say with confidence that joining that Young Adult group was the start of what ultimately led to my freedom from my addiction to sexual sin. That was our church-wide fast at the beginning of 2023.

FASTING AND FREEDOM

The Bible story most will think about when they hear fasting is when Jesus was in the desert for forty days being tempted by the devil. We did not go for forty days without food, we did a modified fast. Because the definition of Fast or Fasting is: The act of abstaining from food. So it doesn't matter what you fast or how much you fast, just as long as you are getting rid of something and replacing it with God. Before the fast started, I went into it wanting real change in my life. Because up until that point, the longest I had gone without doing porn or masturbating was about two weeks. I need a change, a BIG change. So I go through the first week of the fast, and nothing. No porn, no masturbating. I'm getting excited.

Now during the first week of the fast I had asked a girl out, and as we were talking, we started talking about our testimonies, and I felt if this relationship was going to have any chance of success, I needed to tell her I was sexually sinning as soon as it started. The testimony question actually came up when we first "officially" started talking. I say all that to say this girl encouraged me to tell our Young Adult Pastor, since I had only told her and one other person. I initially said I would do it because she asked. But the next morning, I woke up and the Holy Spirit was convicting me about my answer the night before. And then it all came to me. I'm not telling someone because this girl I like asked me to. I'm doing it because I need help. Because I'm sinning. This sin is keeping me from God. It's separating me from God. It's destroying my life, and I'm done having it ruin me. So I immediately texted my pastor, and he agreed to meet with me that afternoon. It was good to tell someone. Because I knew I had someone praying for me, looking out for me, and asking me how I was doing. And he didn't beat around the bush. We would meet weekly, and every time he asked, "Did you look at porn or masturbate this week?" And that's what you need. You need people around you to ask you that straight forward question. Not "how did you do this week" or "did you stumble this week" or "tell me how your week was." Be straight forward, don't beat around the bush. I hate it when people aren't straight forward, especially on a topic like this. Because when you beat around the bush, you're giving whatever the topic is more power than God. Because if you can't be honest, truthful, and straightforward about what it is that's going on and what you're doing, how do you expect to see any change. Change may come, but it will be far longer, or nonexistent.

I know it may be hard to tell someone "I masturbated to this or that on this day last week." It's only going to get easier the more you do it. And if you trust the person you told that you have a sexual sin addiction, then you can trust them with what you did.

So the fast comes and goes, and for twenty-one days straight, no porn or masturbating was present in my life, hallelujah! And the next week, nothing. The next week, nothing again. So I started counting the days. Starting with the beginning of the fast, every day I didn't do porn or masturbate the number would increase by one. I started to feel like a new person. It got to the point when my Pastor would ask me if I had looked at porn or masturbated, I would answer with how many days I had gone without doing either. It was awesome to see during this time that I was still being tempted sexually. But that whenever I was tempted, I would go straight to God. I remember one time I was in a battle for about three hours. Going back and forth, back and forth. And eventually the devil just gave up. HA! He just gave up. But even if he didn't, in the famous words of Captain Rogers: "I can do this all day." And I believe in that moment with the power of God I wouldn't have given in no matter how long that battle was.

So I'm now free from the addiction of porn and masturbating. Is that it? Is that the end of the book? Is the answer to freedom Biblical fasting? Hold the phone there, there's still more to this story. It wasn't until April that I fell back into doing porn and masturbating again. WHAT! I thought you said you found freedom from porn and masturbating! I found freedom from being addicted to it. And may I remind you the Bible tells us we're all sinners. The likely hood of me screwing up and sinning again in my lifetime is an astounding 100%. Now, does that mean that there isn't any freedom from porn and masturbating. No, I don't believe that. I've heard stories of people who were addicted like I was and found freedom, never doing porn or masturbating again. And I believe it's a matter of always having your guard up. Always being ready to fight. I also believe writing this book and bringing back up the memories was a temptation, not one that I would suggest many people do. It's hard to find freedom from sexual sin, and I would argue it's even harder to write about that sexual sin. Relapses shouldn't be taken as an all-out defeat, they should be taken as an opportunity to learn, shake the dust off you, and get back up to continue the fight. So let's walk through why I sinned again.

That Friday was a different Friday than I had had since the fast. It was my first Friday off from work. It was in the middle of March. One hundred and three days I went without doing porn or masturbating. And that Friday I masturbated while lying in bed in the morning. I was devastated. I hated myself. The amount of shame and guilt that plagued me was immense. It was like the devil was chuckling in the corner of whatever room I was in. But I knew exactly why I had done it. Because I hadn't planned what I was going to do that day, when I woke up, I didn't have a goal for the day. I didn't have a purpose. So with nothing to do, nothing to occupy my mind, I just laid in bed. And as I laid in bed, the thoughts just started pouring in. All these sexual thoughts started pouring in until eventually, I decided it was time to masturbate. (In this incident I didn't partake in any form of porn, just masturbating. It wouldn't be until the middle of fall of 2023 that I went back to porn.)

Remember how I talked about when I first looked for the root of the problem, and I thought I was turning to porn because I wasn't being productive. Here this is showing up again. The quicker you pray and ask yourself "why am I turning to porn and masturbating" and get to the root, the far easier it is to see and diagnose what led to you sinning.

And since that Friday in March, I've done porn or masturbated probably a dozen or so times, maybe more. (I have been porn free and masturbating free as of the second week of January 2024. I'll talk more about this in my refection in chapter 15.) But it's far less than what I was doing when I was addicted, and the time between when I sin is far greater. I don't go every day thinking "when am I going to do porn today." Instead it's "I'm going to live for you today God. My body is not my own. I surrender to your will, your commandments." And other days I don't even think about porn (those days are very few and far between).

But every day I'm getting better. Writing this book has been such a help, and I pray it helps you just as much. To know you're not alone, that someone else is doing what you thought you were the only one doing. To know this is a far greater problem than anyone in the church is willing to admit to the congregation and not behind closed doors. You are not alone in this fight. I will be praying that everyone who picks up this book, male and female, can see my story and find that Jesus was the only way to finding freedom. That the journey to freedom is not for the faint of heart, but the blessings that come with freedom are worth the hardship, the pain, the suffering. To not be suicidal, to not be consumed with guilt, to gain your life back. To be yourself again. You may not be the same as you were before, but you will be far stronger than you ever were before. And you can tell your stories of freedom to those that you know. And they can do the same. And before you know it, this will be a fire that spreads across the nation, across the world. I pray that this book starts the discussion the church chose to silence. That they said wasn't for a Sunday morning or a small group. I pray we overtake the culture and expose to them the chains sexual sin cause. That the only freedom is in Christ. That right now there is an epidemic of sexual sin running rampant all over the globe. That if the church won't stand up for it, then the congregation will. I pray there be a change. That small groups start with this book. That it be the pathway to starting these conversations. That any fear people had would be alleviated knowing what I've done. That people would recognize how bad this is and how desperate people are to know the truth. That freedom is possible, but only through Christ.

May You bless this book to the readers, God. To the listeners, to the people who hear about this book. Who pick it up for themselves, for a friend, for a family member, for their churches. May these people find freedom. Have a better understanding of the silent sin in America, in the world. May they have a better understanding of why this sin is so hard and have compassion on those that they know struggle. May those that are sinning have compassion and love on themselves, the same love you, Jesus, showed on the cross. May Your people band together to help each other. To stick with each other through the trenches of this sin. May Your people trust each other and be brave to tell each other what they are going through. And may Your name be glorified when Your people find freedom. Amen.

PART 4:
REFLECTION

AFTERMATH

I really didn't know where to put this last bit of info, so I'll put it here in the aftermath. But throughout my battle with sexual sin, I discovered sex toys on websites. For those that don't know, these are all manner of devices and things that can be used directly or indirectly for sex. I'll just leave it at that. But there were several points throughout my battle that I debated buying some of these sex toys. And this is only because there is an option for what retailers call discreet packaging. This allows your sex toy that you purchased to be shipped in a box that doesn't have any company logo or anything that would indicate what you bought is a sex toy. I find this just a little ironic seeing as sex is considered ok for the world, yet they still offer discreet packaging for those that are embarrassed? I think you can see what I'm getting at.

***

And that's my story. It's one that I'm sure you're hearing for the first time. For some of you there were probably tears as you read this. Tears that you are not alone in your struggle. Tears that you didn't realize the severity of the problem. Tears that this is what a son or daughter is going through. Tears that this is what your husband or wife is going through. Even tears for my broken soul. For some of you there is probably some anger toward the church that we aren't talking about this more. And for some you may be just trying to wrap your mind around the words you just read.

Wherever you are, thank you for taking the time to read my story. The story of a once broken boy that will never fully be the same. A story that is more common than you can even begin to imagine. Thank you for being willing to purchase or borrow this book. This story was very hard to write. And while writing it, I have been in some of my darkest days of my life. The enemy has tried so hard to keep this book from being published; from being in your hands. But God has bigger plans. God's going to do something. So I pray that you would not keep this book to yourself, but you would tell others.

If you got this book for yourself, telling someone you read it is the best starting point. For some of you it may seem impossible to tell others what you've done, what you've experienced. But you could give them this book and say read it all, or read chapter x, y, and z because these include some of the stuff I did or am experiencing. Another starting point would be to have a candid conversation with God about what you've done. And don't hide from what you've done. Be honest. Tell God exactly what you've done. Write out what you've done, talk to a pastor or a trusted friend. Unfortunately, we live in a society where we've been told you can't go to anyone with this sin. You have to do it behind closed doors or with a very trusted friend. So I understand if it's hard to find someone. But you can do it. Paul writes in Romans 8:31 – "What, then, shall we say in response to these things? If God is for us, who can be against us?" and in verse 37 – "Yet in all these things we are more than conquerors through Him who loved us."

If you got this book for a family member, friend, spouse, and/or loved one or were given the book by them, you need to sit down and have that tough conversation with them. The only reason it's tough is because it's new territory for you. But the more you do it the easier it will get. Because if you truly love them, you will suffer to have that conversation with them. You will suffer with them day after day as you check in on them. You will suffer with them because of that hope that today will bring tears, but tomorrow will bring joy and freedom. Because that is unconditional love. That is Godly love.

If you are someone who just picked up this book, thank you. Pass it along to others. Pass it along to your pastor and other leaders of the church. Tell others about it. The more people that know the harder it is to ignore it, especially in the church. And I pray that my story and warnings help and urge you not to give in to sexual temptations.

If you are a leader or a person of influence of any kind. In your house, in your community, in your government, in the world, share this please. Share this with those you know. Let those you lead know about the crisis that is going on behind closed doors. Enact change, call for change, do something. Don't just sit by as human beings, loved ones, fathers, mothers, aunts, uncles, brothers, sisters, children, grandmas, grandpas, doctors, engineers, accountants, fast-food workers, teachers, business owners, are destroying themselves, killing themselves, isolating themselves, cutting themselves, doing drugs, smoking, and so many other things to find relief from what they've done. Who are being changed daily by their actions. Help them. The small guy can start a fire, but you as the accelerant can help it start so much quicker. And others of you may be additional fuel to help the fire last and grow longer. Or you may be the gasoline to make the flame huge.

Together we can inform parents, grandparents, guardians, teachers, we can inform everyone of the devastating nature of porn use and masturbating has on us. We can stop grade schoolers being exposed to porn at such a young age. We can stop the high school addict from taking their life because they feel so alone. We can stop the father from taking his life because he sees the pain in his wife's eyes every time he tells her he sinned sexually. We can stop the girls who grew up in church only hearing sexual sin was a man's problem, thinking something is wrong with them because they are a woman who sexually sins. We can stop the one-week addicts, the one-month addicts, the six-month addicts, the one-year addicts, the two-year addicts, the five-year addicts, the ten-year addicts, the fifteen-year addicts, the twenty-year addicts, and beyond.

But we can only do it together. And we can only do it if you agree this needs to stop.

2nd Relapse

As much as it kills me to say this, as of the writing of this (September of 2023), I have unfortunately fallen back into being addicted to porn and masturbating. This is why we need to be more open, not be afraid to discuss sexual sin openly. Be willing to stick with people who are recovering and help them when they relapse, so it doesn't go back to being an addiction. I can say that I know exactly why it happened. I didn't keep up with my accountability partners when they stopped checking as regularly, I kept my electronics far too close to me bed, I stopped reading my Bible as frequently, and I let the events going on in my life get me in a state of depression that I turned right back to porn and masturbating.

I let the events in my life as well as falling back into sexual sin lead to the first genuine time that I was suicidal. I remember a lot was going on at the time. Physically, mentally, relationally, everything I felt like was wrong, off, not where it should be. And it all came to a head one Wednesday. I don't like remembering that day very much, but I know this story will save someone, or give them hope.

My mind had been racing that day. And very early on that Wednesday I remember telling myself "I want to kill myself." I didn't know how I was going to do it, just that it was going to happen. But at the same time I was replying to that statement with "NO YOU DON'T!" or "JESUS LOVES YOU. He died for you! You have so much to offer this world!" And this fight played out in my head all day. And of that day there are two moments I still remember, the rest are lost in my mind. The first, I had just left the store after buying some knee braces. (My knees had always hurt me and with my job at the time, it was causing them to hurt really bad, far more often and far more severe than ever before. Even to the point where every time I would squat down a sharp pain went up the inside of my right knee.) I had to get a smaller size because the bigger ones kept sliding off my knees. I had been to the Young Adult group, and someone made a comment on my knee braces that really rubbed me the wrong way, a comment about "was I going to play soccer," and something about knee pads. A comment that any other day I would have laughed along with them. But that stuck out to me for some reason a week later, and I felt like such a misfit. I had a broken body. And it was there that I said or thought something to the degree of "God, I'm going to go through with this if you don't do something. You know me, you know how I am." (I'm not entirely sure if that is anywhere near close to what I thought, so please forgive me if that is not what I said, but I don't remember that well.)

So later that night I go to my Young Adults group at church, wearing the knee braces (with shorts, so everyone could see). And that night we talked about being single (which was one of the things my mind decided wasn't right with me, that I was single, alone, and still dealing with a past break-up). So we go through the night, and we have prayer time for anyone that wanted it. So people stand at the front of the room, and we all disperse to pray for these individuals. And right after I had finished praying for someone, my good friend William finished praying next to me and asked me how I was doing. All I said was, "Not good."

Immediately, he went into prayer with me. He prayed fervently, sincerely, and all I could do was listen. It was a very intimate time between us, it's hard for me to describe exactly what the experience was like. But I remember at one point our foreheads were together and I thought, "Normally this would weird me out, but surprisingly, it doesn't whatsoever." There was such a deep love between us, a brotherly love, a Godly love. And by the end of that prayer, I didn't want to kill myself. All those feelings, emotions, thoughts, completely and utterly gone. And no, I didn't fall down on the ground convulsing, or slain in the spirit, or collapse, or see stars or a bright light, I didn't feel all tingly inside. There was nothing. Nothing whatsoever. When the prayer started, I was suicidal. When the prayer ended, I was not suicidal.

And all I can say to that is that's the love and power of God right there. Hallelujah and amen!

Now something interesting I'd like to note, I wrote a poem as I was sitting in the parking lot, waiting to go into the Young Adults group. And that poem is as follows:

The Fight Inside

This is the fight
That happens every waking hour
That no one knows

No one can see
Cause I don't let them
I say I can do it on my own

And when I want to tell you
I don't
and put on my fake face

And without a word
I kill myself again
because I can't be honest

I can't be true
And that's all I want
to be true

BONDAGE TO FREEDOM

But the enemy strikes
and breaks my defenses
like a crumbling cookie

Leaving fire and ash
in their wake

And once again
the fight is on

This time is easier
for them
They broke everything before

I have nothing left

Just this soul
and whatever is left inside

So the enemy surrounds me

beaten
broken
breathless

I won't surrender
I said last time
This time I'm quiet

But just as the killing blow begins

there You are

In my desperate hour
In my hopelessness
You shine through

You blind the enemy
You drive them back
You free me

You're so bright
even the shadows hide

And as the hour becomes still
quiet
I have no words

I know your question
before it leaves Your lips
Why did you lose hope?

I fall to my knees
and weep

You wrap me in a hug
There, there child
You say

And all I can do
Is say I'm sorry

But you lift my head
to show me the reminder
I see Your hand
and the light shining through

I nearly cried writing that out. Wow. In the face of utter despair and hopeless-ness, I still clung to Jesus. I really don't know what more I can say on that.

What I will say is thank you, William, for your prayers. You saved my life that day. I wrote that poem on 9/13/23 (September 13, 2023). Because of your prayers, William, I get to share my story today. Thank you!

And that is why you need Godly friends. Friends who will pray for you, intervene for you, be an accountability partner. This is why it's key to be able to identify or have someone else identify what is causing you to sexually sin, so you can act accordingly and not in vain. So let's dive into how you can act here in the next chapter.

TECHNIQUES FOR FREEDOM

1) Prayer – For those of you reading that have not accepted Jesus as their Lord and Savior, this is your opportunity. Because the Bible tells us that it is only by the power of God that the desires of us humans are able to be put in check. It is not by our strength, but by God's that you will ever find freedom from sexual sin. You can try all these techniques that I share, that God and other Christ following people shared with me, and you may very well find freedom. I guarantee you there are stories out there of people who aren't Christian having never done porn or masturbating or found freedom from porn and masturbating. But they're not doing it for Christ. They're not doing it because as a follower of Christ that is how He commands us to live, sexually pure lives. Because our lives are in God's hands. When we die, we will either live in eternity with God or be sentenced to hell. And God tells us in John 3:16 "For God so solved the world that He gave his only begotten Son, that whoever believes in him should not perish but have everlasting life." So I give you the opportunity now to declare Jesus as your Lord and Savior. That he died on the cross for your sins, paying the ultimate price and being the final sacrifice, that you may have the opportunity to accept him and be given the gift of eternal life. All you have to do is what John 3:16 says, believe. The American church has decided that you have to repeat after them a prayer of confession that Jesus is the son of God and that he died for your sins to give you the gift of eternal life. But I believe God wants us to come as we are to him and talk to him from our own mouth, not repeat something from someone else's mouth. All prayer is, is talking to God. So pray to God to tell him that you believe in his son Jesus. I guarantee you it is the best decision of your life. Because when you follow God, your life improves ten-fold. It may not look like it. It will take time to change (sometimes a very long time to change), but it does. Look at my life. I was doing porn, masturbating, suicidal, and depressed. Now I'm finding healing from all of those, as well as many more (sounds like another book).

Now for those of you that are already following God, you just need to start praying. Pray for forgiveness from your sin and repent. Look up verses in the Bible about sexual sin so you understand that what you are doing is sinful. Pray for help because you alone will never defeat this sin. Pray for God to put people in your life that you can go to for help. Pray to have the strength to confess your sins to those people, so they can help you in the healing process. Pray for wisdom for why you are turning to porn and masturbating. Is it an underlying problem you've never dealt with that's causing this behavior, or is it a release from stress, anxiety, etc. Pray that you would hate sexual sin. Your flesh may like it, even crave it, but pray that your spirit would be strengthened to resist your flesh and want to glorify God. Pray that you may surrender your fleshly desires to God. Pray that you fully surrender yourself to God, that you surrender all to Him.

Prayer is powerful. Ask others to pray the same things you are.

2) Accountability Partner – Still to this day when I hear this phrase it has a negative connotation in my mind. But it's not. This goes back to James 5:16 – "Confess your trespasses to one another, and pray for one another." Find someone you know and tell them what you've done and ask for them to check up on you, ask if you've sexually sinned at all. Now most people would say find someone you know and trust as well as someone who is the same gender as you. Unfortunately for some of you, you may not have someone in your life that you trust. And according to James 5:16, it doesn't say to confess your trespasses to people you trust. Or confess your sins to those of the same gender. It says Confess your sins to one another. For the Americans reading this, this will be hard to swallow. Because the American church is already very secretive about sexual sin, but it also thinks that men should only confess to men and the women should only confess to women. Even overseas when dealing with sexual trafficking victims, one company only employs women to council women, and don't council any men (more likely boys) for some reason. This company came and spoke at my church. I was talking with one of the representatives afterword and questioned them about not seeing any way that men could help the victims. And their answer was that they don't let men council the women who have been trafficked. THIS IS COMPLETELY BONKERS! I was offering my help, and you deny me because of my gender. For what reason. You think I'll hurt them just by looking at them? You think I'll be too forceful or some other absurd reason? You expect these women you save and rescue to be able to reacclimate to society in any reasonable manner when they've been secluded from men for the duration of their time with you. What are you afraid of? I understand that if a man raped these women who are being trafficked, they may not want to see a man again. But you don't believe that the love of Jesus Christ can shine through a man and break down those barriers these women may have put up in their lives. And what if a woman was raped by another woman. Well your whole argument falls apart. And don't tell me that men can't be raped and that's why you don't council or hire men. We need to stop dividing what is "appropriate" to converse about by gender and reunite the church to be living as James 5:16 commands.

Having an accountability partner will also grow each of your relationship together if both of you are Christians. You can even have an accountability partner for things not related to sexual sin. It can be for anything that you may have a bad habit of falling into or something that you don't want to fall into.

3) Memorizing Bible Verses – When you memorize Bible verses, it's amazing what happens when you start repeating those while being tempted. There is a confidence that can't be shaken when the devil is tempting you to sexually sin, but you're speaking God's word right back and saying no. It also will help replace any thoughts of sexually sinning with God. Now any Bible verse is better than none. But there are specific verses that will help more than others, like those that pertain to sexual sin. Currently my arsenal of verses includes 1 Corinthians 6:18-20, Psalm 51:10, and Job 31:1 all in the NKJV. So whenever I'm tempted, I will say these verses, repeat them, and do as they say. I've also found that simply defining a few words and analyzing these verses can better help you understand them. For example. I took very brief notes on Job 31:1 which says: "I have made a covenant with my eyes; why then should I look upon a young woman." I looked up the definition for covenant which was: an agreement. And then I did some thinking about the term young woman writing, "acknowledges physical beauty in youth. But true beauty is found in the heart of the beholder." That beauty is a love for Christ, a love that rises above all relationships.

Now for those of you worried or afraid about the concept of memorizing verses, it's not that hard. Growing up, I was horrible at memorizing for tests and whatnot at school. So when memorizing these verses, my Young Adult Pastor suggested I write the verses down on index cards and carry them around. This helped a lot as I had just the verse in front of me, not all the other verses surrounding it as I would when memorizing it from the Bible directly. I wasn't so easily distracted. And these index cards went into my little notebook I carry around with me. So I've always got them on hand to reference when need be.

I'm sure there are a thousand other memorizing techniques out there, so use whichever one works best for you.

4) Electronics Accountability – This is by far the easiest and the hardest on the list of techniques. As in my story, I got rid of my smartphone and replaced it with a flip-phone. For some of you this may be super easy, and for others it will be the hardest thing for you. But it's worth it if it means you will have freedom. On top of that, take out all the electronic devices in the room where you consume your porn. (For most this will be your bedroom. If you are living by yourself, this is where an accountability partner could take your electronic devices from you. And if you need them for work, it may be a case of you have to leave it on the opposite end of the house. This is where prayer and friends/accountability partners will come in handy with how to deal with your specific situation.).

5) Other Erotic Accountability – This is similar to electronics accountability but dealing with all other things that may turn you on. This includes sex toys (if you used them or have them/have access to them), not sex toys that are sex toys (devices/objects that are not by definition a sex toy but used as one or used to recreate sexual intercourse/acts in any way), photos used to masturbate to, locations visited where sexual acts took/take place and/or sexually arouse you (strip clubs, sex shops, places you and an old boyfriend/girlfriend would meet, where you and someone partook in sexual acts, beaches, going out to gawk at people with the hopes of being sexually aroused, etc.), and anything else that may sexually arouse you that can be removed from your dwelling and lifestyle. Again, friends/accountability partners that you are open and completely honest with can help you with your specific situation.

6) Praying away spirits/demons – Depending on how severe and how long your addiction is, you could be dealing with a demonic force, such as an evil spirit or demon. This will take fervent prayer and the prayer of many. I started off by anointing my bedroom door frame (where I partook in my sexual sin the most) with oil and in the name of Jesus rebuked any evil spirits from my room. I also prayed against any spirits attached to me and rebuked them in the name of Jesus. Your church will be a great place to start for finding people to help pray with you. Some people may even have performed an exorcism before and can do the same for you. That may sound scary but continuing to sin and live against God's command; continuing to sin and thinking about every time I sin the nails being slammed into Jesus hands and feet is my fault. I fear that far more than an exorcism.

7) Become involved in Church – Getting involved in the church is a great help. It will start you building relationships that can turn into accountability partners. It will occupy your time, so you don't have as much of it to be tempted by. And getting involved in your church will help keep the church thriving, as well as allow you to utilize the gifts and talents God has given you to benefit His people.

CONSEQUENCES

And here's the chapter you won't hear in too many places. What are the consequences of doing porn, masturbating, and other sexual sin. Because I guarantee you, if I had known the consequences, I would have been far more hesitant to do my own research and get to the point that I am today.

Initial Consequences

- I sinned

- The first time I made myself ejaculate and orgasm was not having sex with my wife

- I cried

- The amount of shame my actions created

- The amount of guilt my actions created

- I felt dirty

- I felt like an animal

- I felt unworthy before God

Continued/ongoing Consequences

- I continue sinning

- I feel unworthy before God sometimes

- The amount of shame I carry

- The amount of guilt I carry

- Not wanting to read my Bible after sinning sexually

- Sitting in my shame and being lazy all day right after sexually sinning

- Not writing books after sexually sinning

- Having suicidal thoughts

- Wanting to commit suicide

- Wanting to run as far away from God as possible

- Ejaculating and having an orgasm far quicker than when I first started masturbating

- Having a hyper sexualized mind:

  - Jokes that used to fly over me, I now get

  - Thinking or fantasizing about porn, masturbating, etc. randomly throughout the day

  - No longer being innocent and pure in thought

- Beating myself up over my sin when God has already forgiven me

- Worrying about a girl not going out with me or a girlfriend breaking up with me over my sexual sin

Future/possible Consequences

- Will I ever find full freedom?

- Will I commit suicide from all the shame and guilt I carry?

- How will my sexual sin affect dating?

- Will I want/be able to ask a woman out or will I feel unworthy of dating because of my sexual sin

- How will my sexual sin affect my marriage?

- Will I want to have sex with my wife?

- Will I have no sex drive or a low sex drive with my wife?

- Will I have a super high sex drive that is unrealistic because of the consistency and frequency that I partook in porn and masturbating?

- Will my wife always be wondering what I'm thinking of her body?

- Will my wife change her body, attitude, clothing, etc. to fit the kind of porn I liked?

- Will my wife always be concerned that I love her after what I've done?

- Will I react negatively if when I have sex with my wife, it doesn't meet the expectations I have from the porn I watched, read, or listened/heard?

- Will I develop erectile dysfunction or other sexual/body dysfunctions, both mental and physical from my addiction?

- Will I lose friends if they find out what I've done?

- Will family reject me if they find out what I've done?

- Will anyone marry me?

- Will I lose my job if co-workers find out what I've done?

- Once people know what I've done, will I be able to make any new friends/relationships?

- Will God ever take away the thoughts, images, urges, and anything else that came from my sexual sin, or will he heal me and make me the innocent little boy I used to be?

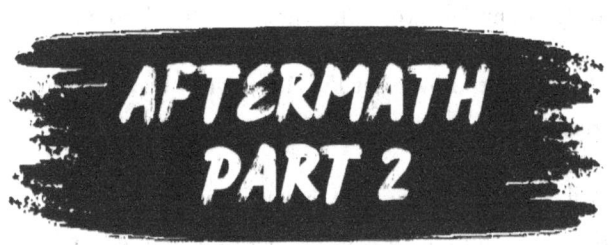

AFTERMATH PART 2

This book took far longer to write than I expected. What should have been two-to-three months turned into almost a year. A big part of that was this fear that I would fall back into sexual sin while writing it. And that is a very fair and valid fear to have. Anyone who digs up their past that they had put away and dealt with should be cautious looking back into it as extensively as I did.

Now you already know that I had relapsed after 103 days by masturbating. A relapse is not something that needs to be a four-alarm fire level of attention. It does deserve your attention like I discussed. But when I finally got back to editing and writing this book in October of 2023, it was like I was back in 2020 again. I started watching video porn again, masturbating, and reading erotica about two-to-three times a week at its height.

It wasn't until around my Christmas break that I stopped and considered why I had fallen back into sexual sin so hard. And it all clicked for me when I was watching a new movie. In the middle of it was a brief sex scene that I was unaware of. It was less than two seconds, no one was naked, no words were said, just one person starting to initiate sex. And the next thing I know, that night I went and watched some porn and masturbated.

Now the next day the Holy Spirit was helping me realize that I no longer had control of myself if an erotic scene came on. Growing up, if there was an erotic scene that my parents didn't realize was in a movie, we would skip that scene immediately. If I had the remote, even I would immediately skip it. But since 2020, I would either partake in the erotic scene, or go searching out movies and shows with erotic content. So during the last two weeks of 2023 and the first week of 2024, I made mental notes about what movies and books to get rid of.

Along with this list I made a list of media I had that wasn't uplifting either. A lot of this included music that was depressing, and when thinking about it more, this music actually kept me in a very depressed state in regards with something else that happened to me in 2023. But when I started relapsing more and more during this time, that only added to the already depressed state I was in. So in short (because I could go on forever about the impact of what media we consume does to us), if the media and music you listen to is not Christian, hopeful, or positive, you really need to have a come to Jesus meeting about continuing to indulge in that type of media, critically analyzing if it's changing your life in a positive or negative way.

Now back to my list of media I needed to get rid of, it wasn't until the third week of this process (the first week in January 2024) that I was able to bag everything up and get rid of it (some if it thrown away because it was too erotic). It took me until the third week because it was hard for my flesh to let go of all this entertainment, most of which I enjoyed and had bought myself.

But when I finally got rid of it, my spirit was satisfied and rejoiced, while my flesh screamed for me to turn back. But since then, I haven't partaken in porn or masturbated, and I feel much more free. I don't have to worry now about watching a movie or TV show I own and having in the back of my mind the question of will that scene make me fall back into the sin again. It's worth the pain that it cost because the benefits far outweigh the negative.

But that's the hard part about living in a life saying no more to sexual sin addiction. There were things I was able to do growing up, that because I was addicted for so long, I can no longer do anymore. And that's what you won't hear a lot of, the lifelong aftereffects of being addicted to sexual sin. It's an unfortunate reality that if more people knew, I guarantee would make people more guarded to sexual sin. Which is the ultimate goal for writing this book, to warn you about ALL the dangers that come with sexual sin, and demonstrate why the Bible is so direct with abstaining from sexual sin.

But even with all the dangers, even with the changes to my life, even with everything I don't know going forward, even with my innocence lost, even with the acts I've done that will never see the light of day, there is still good to be found in this situation.

1) I am alive: As you read previously, there were several times where were it not for my faith in God, or the prayers of my brother in Christ, I would not be writing this book today. This book would not be in your hands. I would be dead. But that is not the case. Because that is how powerful God is.

2) When I am living for God, I feel no shame or guilt for my past: This is probably one that still amazes/puzzles me the most when I sit down and really dwell on it. That I can go through an entire day without being ashamed of my past demonstrates the grace and love that God has for His creation.

3) I was able, willing, and wanting to write this book: It's not every day that someone writes a book on their past sin, especially sexual sin. There were days where I didn't want to write this book, to release it to the world. I wanted to destroy it and move on to other works. I would freak out over the potential consequences for writing this book. But every time one of those fears creeped in, it wasn't long before those fears were gone, and I thought about the boy who didn't know how to be free from his shame of sexual sin. Or the girl that suffers silently because she's grown up being told porn and masturbating are a man's problem, never a woman's problem. Those are the people I write for. They are the ones I pray this book reaches. And that drowns out all the fear. And again, that's the power of God.

4) I had God move in such a personal way in my life: To have experienced and know the love of God in such a personal way is something that I truly treasure. And it's something that I hope I captured to some proportion for you.

Now I could go on and on about all the positives, but I'll leave it with those above.

I pray my story has given you hope, and shown you or a loved one how to find freedom from sexual sin, specifically porn and masturbating. I pray that you would recognize God is the only one that can save you, and for those that haven't accepted Him, choose to accept Him as your Lord and Savior. Go in peace. Go in FREEDOM! AMEN!

FINAL REMARKS

Since that day I have not been the same. I was no longer the innocent young man who knew nothing about female anatomy (I was never shown the female anatomy in health class or any other class in school), who didn't know anything about sex except how to do it and that's how humans reproduced. I didn't know what a condom was and that it was used so your wife wouldn't get pregnant, who didn't know you could have sex more than just when you wanted to reproduce, who didn't know there was great pleasure involved with sex (orgasm), who when he first saw a vagina thought "That's not at all what I imagined, that can't be right," who wanted to be a virgin and share his wedding bed with his wife and make having sex for the first time pure and innocent as God intended (I have not had sexual intercourse with another woman, but I believe that after masturbating and partaking in porn I am no longer a virgin), who felt like and still feels like an animal knowing the things I did and how I masturbated, who will never be that innocent little boy ever again who knew only how to have sex.

But through God, I have found Freedom, I have found grace, I have found purpose. I pray you find the same.

He who covers his sins will not prosper, But whoever confesses and forsakes them will have mercy – Proverbs 28:13

If this book impacted you in any way I would love to hear from you. You can contact me at my website eecooley.com. Your messages of hope not only encourage me but also others as I share the impact this book has had on those who read it.

If after reading this you would like me to come speak on *Bondage to Freedom*, or any of the subjects discussed in the book (pornography, masturbating, suicide, sexual sin, etc.) you can also contact me at eecooley.com to book me for your event. All my speaking engagements are free to you. You read that right, I won't charge a penny, I just want the opportunity to speak to your church, small group, community, etc. on the silent sin in America.

After dropping out of college to publish his first book Prime Youth: Prisoners of the Masquerade, E.E. hasn't put his pen down. And with too many ideas to count he won't be putting that pen down anytime soon. When he has to force himself to stop writing he does the next best thing, reading. He also enjoys hiking and is actively involved in his home church, ensuring E.E. has a steady stream of inspiration and friends to help him along his journey.

Website: eecooley.com

Instagram: @e.e.cooley

Facebook: E.E. Cooley

Twitter: @EE_Cooley